Writing Pictures K-12:
A Bridge to Writing Workshop

D1511320

Writing Pictures K-12:
A Bridge to Writing Workshop

Hal and Michelle Takenishi

Christopher-Gordon Publishers, Inc.
Norwood, Massachusetts

Credits

Every effort has been made to contact copyright holders for permission to reproduce borrowed material where necessary. We apologize for any oversights and will be happy to rectify them in future printings.

All student work used with permission.

Publishers Note: Throughout this book the authors have encouraged readers to adapt the forms to suit the needs of their classrooms.

The Bill Harp Professional Teacher's Library
An Imprint of
Christopher-Gordon Publishers, Inc.
1502 Providence Highway, Suite #12
Norwood, MA 02062
(800) 934-8322

Printed in the United States of America

10 9 8 7 6 5 4 3 2 1   04 03 02 01 00 99

Library of Congress Catalog Card Number: 98-073521
ISBN: 0-926842-88-9

Contents

The Blob

I grabbed Adam's flab in the water and tugged lightly. My throat filled with water from his splashes and I could feel him struggling to get away. As I grabbed an even tighter grip on his pot belly, he persisted. "So you want more," I taunted, spinning him around, and catching him back in a giant bear hug.

Around his waist my arms went, and I lifted him up as high as I could. My spine bent backward and I could smell the chlorine in the water. "Now I gotcha'. Right where I want you," I panted. Getting ready, I cocked back my waist, spun around, pushed him back while releasing him, and threw him in the air.

Nicholas

Did an elementary school student write this in a regular classroom?

Yes.

Is he a gifted student?

No.

Could he write like this from the beginning of school?

No.

How was he taught to write like this?

INTRODUCTION

"I don't have time to teach writing!"

"I don't know how."

"I give them time, choice, and ownership and, still, my kids show little improvement."

"I need to work on grammar and spelling."

"I have too many other subjects that need to be focused on."

Do all those statements sound familiar? As dedicated teachers, we slaved at the teaching of writing. We attended yearly conventions, read masses of literature, enrolled in classes, and still saw minimal progress. As we saw it, the good kids stayed good, the average kids stayed average, and the slow kids stayed slow. There were "moments" of course, but, overall, the writing stayed the same.

We agonized for hours searching for answers. We gave the kids an hour each day, diligently conducted mini-lessons, read literature and picture story books to them, conducted writing conferences until our heads spun, read each student's piece (at times, 10 pages long) carefully, and tried to honor all students at their level. Still, we saw minimal results.

The unavoidable reality hit us. We didn't know HOW to teach writing. We could give them as much time, choice and ownership as needed, but to actually help them develop was beyond us. We needed to rethink what we were doing. Slowly, a simple, daily writing exercise evolved.

Writing Pictures, henceforth called pictures, is a **FOUR SENTENCE** daily developmental exercise. Beginning with LEVEL ONE, the students are taken through the basic format, and, with time, progress upward through LEVEL SIX. With each successive level, students are expected to write with more sophistication and attention to detail.

The heart of pictures focuses on having the students visualize one moment in their life of their own choosing, sketch it quickly, and write four guided sentences in paragraph format about it.

It should be emphasized that pictures is a daily exercise similar to practicing scales on the piano. It should not be confused with actual stories or process writing, nor should it become the entire writing program.

Once introduced, the whole process can take a minimum of thirty minutes. Should the teacher want to incorporate other skills, such as grammar, vocabulary, spelling and reading skills, more time can be given. Although the choice of topic is the child's, heavy teacher guidance is given as to the construction of the paragraph.

Almost four years ago, we began putting our ideas into practice. With time and much discussion among other teachers that crossed several grade levels, we put together a systematic, developmental approach that helps both teacher and student feel more confident.

What Are the Benefits of this Writing Approach?

1. It makes the teacher feel secure and confident.

   Teachers will be able to adjust the lesson to make it harder or easier, slower or faster, according to their own program and needs.

2. All students, from slow to gifted, develop confidently at their own individual pace.

   Students are encouraged to think of pictures from their own lives on a daily basis. Whether they need to have teacher assistance, peer tutoring, or simply more time, students progress at their own pace privately.

3. All students understand what the exact process is and, because of that, understand how to self-correct.

   Students know exactly what is expected of them from each sentence and are unafraid of the blank page. This leads to confidence and the beginning of how to approach revision.

4. Grammar, language, vocabulary and spelling skills can be reinforced daily and weekly within their own writing.

   The teacher can choose to incorporate the teaching of parts of speech, punctuation skills, spelling, vocabulary and oral reading.

5. Over time, other types of writing can be expanded from this one paragraph, four sentence approach.

   Pictures can be used as a tool to help revise longer pieces of writing.

6. Teachers understand how to get mini-lessons from the writings of their students.

   Mini-lesson needs quickly surface as the students write; the teacher can then decide which of them needs to be attended to and at what pace.

7. Written work done by students quickly shows focus.

   Because the students are writing only four sentences, they are able to focus themselves on exactly what is being asked of them in each sentence.

8. Writing accountability and assessment are high since tests are given once a week.

   One paragraph following the pictures format is expected a minimum of once a week. Performance in spelling, punctuation, proper grammar and use of vocabulary counts toward the student's grade. Students approach this test confidently since it is practiced daily and it serves as a useful tool to measure their writing progress.

9. Language and grammar skills are emphasized through mini-lessons and reinforced through personalized skill lists.

   With each lesson and test, the teacher is continuously made aware of the types of mini-lessons needed. Some need to be dealt with as a class and some need only a private reminder.

10. Connections to literature are made continuously.

    Students are strongly encouraged to use higher vocabulary and search through literature for examples of good writing.

Although we are certainly not saying that WRITING PICTURES will be the panacea to all writing difficulties, it has been our experience that it gives students and teachers confidence in their efforts toward improving writing.

We hope that this book helps you to look at the teaching of writing from another perspective.

Dedication

To Ann Ing, Terry Ishihara, SheilaNono and Carolyn Goo
for their unwavering faith that
this book would find an audience.

To our daughter, Sherry—our lucky charm.

Basic Overview

To help make your first day successful, here are some things to remember. Any detailed questions you may have about exactly how to prepare prior to your first day will be discussed in the next section.

1. Pictures is a daily writing exercise that takes approximately 30 minutes a day.

2. It uses only *four (4) sentences* to form a complete paragraph.

3. Within the first week, most students will be able to write *one concise, complete paragraph.*

4. Supplies — one marble black and white tablet
   — one manila folder with name and number assigned to each student
   — see page xv for more details

5. Allow for one hour on the first day to leisurely introduce "writing pictures."

   Subsequent lessons should take *approximately half an hour per day;* 10 minutes for the initial mini-lesson, with written work by students taking the remaining 20 minutes. Don't hesitate to allow more time if necessary.

6. This approach requires students to quickly sketch a different moment from their own life each day, to help them visualize. The actual illustration drawn should not take more than a few minutes. *Stick figures only,* no colors, 2–3 minutes maximum.

   Lower grades will take longer. Initially, illustrations should be real, taken from their own lives, and should include themselves. Give them time to color their illustrations and draw with more care. This is part of their writing process. The illustration may be done as homework.

In the K-1 level, pictures should begin as a class exercise and move into individual exercises, only if the teacher feels students are capable of handling it.

Secondary schools—time is a factor. Illustrations as well as four sentence written exercise could be assigned as daily homework.

7. Pictures is progressive through six levels, based upon how your students develop. Although it is recommended that you stay at each level a minimum of one month to give them ease and confidence, don't hesitate to stay at each level for a longer or shorter period of time. Go at whatever pace makes you feel comfortable.

    In each level, reinforce higher-level vocabulary usage, proper grammar and punctuation, spelling issues, beginning in different ways, "show" details.

8. A short 5- to 10-minute mini-lesson can be taught daily to reinforce what is being introduced. Mini-lesson ideas can be found in Appendix A.

    Mini-lessons can be new, or based upon grammatical concerns you notice. They can also be simple and short, such as reminding the class to include their date and indent upon beginning.

    A good rule of thumb is to present two or three new mini-lessons within one week. The mini-lessons on remaining days can be simple reminders to do such things as remember to double check what they have written.

9. Initially, each Pictures tablet can be looked at daily as you take a simple walk around to monitor students' progress. With time, you will find it unnecessary to look at all of the tablets daily, and you will be able to choose when, and which tablets, if any, you want to look at for closer inspection.

10. Weekly tests or quizzes can be given once a week for accountability.

11. *Punctuation* concerns will be dealt with through weekly tests, quizzes, class mini-lessons, and/or individual skill sheets.

12. *Vocabulary and Spelling* concerns will be dealt with through literature. Variations and choices will be discussed further in this book.

GETTING READY

When to Begin

Pictures should be emphasized from the first day of school. We like to begin on the first day of the school year to emphasize the importance of reading and writing in our curriculum.

If you find it difficult to begin on the first day of school, it is perfectly acceptable to begin at another time when you feel more comfortable, such as the beginning of another quarter or semester. Whenever you choose to begin could then become your chosen "first day."

Beginning on the first day helps you to use pictures as an assessment of each student's writing capabilities. The discerning teacher, later in the day, can look through the tablets and notice handwriting, punctuation, vocabulary, spelling, sense of story, and independent working skills. This also sets up the basic philosophy of writing daily that you want to emphasize from the very beginning.

Supplies Needed

1. *A tablet.* Each student should have a tablet for their daily written work. We like to use a black and white marble composition tablet because its pages do not come out easily.

2. *A manila folder.* Each student will need a blank manila folder with holes punched at the top on both sides with prongs inserted. The student's name and number should be clearly labeled for easier storing and retrieving.

3. *A designated place for tablets.*   As tablets are used, there should be a designated spot for tablets to be picked up and returned by class leaders.

4. *A scheduled time.*   A minimum of half an hour should be set aside daily at the same time so that students have the same routine every day. You can lengthen or shorten the time assigned to pictures according to your needs.

Once you have decided how to schedule your day to accommodate pictures, you need to decide what time block you will allocate to writing each day. Again, it is important to remember that you must have a minimum of half an hour of uninterrupted time daily.

We like to use times such as first thing in the morning, after lunch, or after recess. We suggest having sustained silent reading, reading workshop, or some quiet period of independent work immediately following writing so that time will be available to conference with those few students who seem to need a bit more clarification.

Scheduling

Sample Schedule (A)

7:50—Morning business. Usual morning routine.

8:30—Math

9:30—**PICTURES****

10:05—Recess

10:25—Reading Workshop

11:30—Content Curriculum/other writing genre

12:00—Lunch

12:30—Content Curriculum/other writing genre

2:05—Dismissal

**We are assuming that the opening lesson for pictures, which can span one day or several weeks, has already been attended to. This sample schedule is for the daily exercise of pictures once the schedule has been set.

Content curricula such as science or social studies have been placed within an integrated schedule.

Sample Schedule (B)—Self-Contained Classroom

This schedule applies to Monday, Wednesday, Thursday and Friday. Tuesday is set aside for all other content such as Music, Art, P.E., Social Studies, Health, and Science.

In this way, we can have large chunks of time available for teaching reading and writing as separate subjects, integrating as we feel necessary.

7:50—**PICTURES.** No mini-lesson at this time, since it will be taught during writing workshop later in the day. Students should come to school prepared to write.

8:05—Morning business

8:15—Math

9:15—Teacher reads literature/conducts mini-lessons

10:05—Recess

10:30—Mini-lessons (content areas—vocabulary)

11:00—Reading Workshop

12:00—Lunch

12:30—**PICTURES.** Formal mini-lessons (see Appendix A) by the teacher should be taught here. Students should be given time to write immediately thereafter.

1:00—Writing Workshop

2:05—Dismissal

Sample Schedule (C)—Departmentalized

7:50—**PICTURES.** No mini-lesson at this time, since it will be taught during writing workshop later in the day. Students should come to school prepared to write.

8:05—Morning business

8:15—Continuation of pictures; teacher teaches mini-lesson

8:45—Content curriculum—different subject each day

10:05—Recess

10:30—Math

11:15—Writing Workshop (separate from "Pictures")

12:00—Lunch

12:30—Reading Workshop

1:15—Content Integration

2:05—Dismissal

On Tuesdays, we stop the teaching of math, reading and writing as separate subjects. We reserve that day for reflection, researching, individual student academic pursuits, and furthering inquiry-based learning.

Daily Mini-lessons using Schedules (B) and (C)

If you choose to use Schedule (A) for your class, you will have no problem with conducting your mini-lessons at the scheduled time.

If, however, you choose to follow Schedule (B) or Schedule (C), the second and third sample schedules outlined above, it gets a bit confusing since the morning begins with pictures. In this situation, you *cannot* begin with a mini-lesson. The requirement of a mini-lesson being administered daily still holds, but it must now wait until your formal pictures writing time.

Confused?

We have a rule in our classroom that states, "Students must be ready and writing BEFORE the bell rings." According to Harry and Rosemary Wong, the bell doesn't begin class nor does the teacher. The students begin class.[*]

In keeping with that principle, our students are at their seat and writing pictures, usually beginning about 10 minutes before the bell rings. It's pretty amazing.

We want to emphasize the importance of writing and the premise that students should come to school prepared to write. Because the students are writing before the bell, we do not give a mini-lesson when the bell rings. We stop temporarily for the flag

---

[*]Harry K. Wong and Rosemary T. Wong, *The First Days of School: How to Be an Effective Teacher.* Sunnyvale, CA: Harry K. Wong Publications, 1991.

pledge, song, announcements, and then give them about 10 more minutes.

Our students work hard during this time. It is only during our scheduled pictures block of time during writing workshop that we begin the period with a formal mini-lesson.

You do not need to have this morning period of pictures. It is just as wonderful to have half an hour of an allotted pictures time during any other period within your schedule. However, always remember to begin with some type of mini-lesson. We will discuss types of mini-lessons at greater length on pages 27–31. If you stick to this, your students will continue to grow.

Laminated/Posted Handout

It is suggested that handout Level ONE, Appendix B, be xeroxed and pasted inside each student tablet for easy reference.

If you choose not to use the handout Level ONE, be sure to emphasize the format daily so that the students become familiar with it.

Spelling

Last, but most important, address the issue of spelling. There are many schools of thought about spelling but most published manuscripts, literature, and research seem to point to one basic issue. Spelling should come from the students' own work.

We have experimented with spelling in many ways. We've learned that if we say spelling counts only at various moments, the students will not honor the need to always look at their work carefully. Therefore, we say that spelling counts all the time in every subject area. This dramatically cuts down on the number of times the question, "Does spelling count"?, is raised.

Although there are no clear-cut ways to handle this issue, here are a few ways in which spelling might be handled within the classroom.

Choice 1 "Frequently misspelled words," Appendix C, numbering 70 words, could be given as a spelling test and graded once a week. We know that 70 may seem a lot; however, we make extensive use of peer testing as well as peer grading. Once students have an "A," thus demonstrating competency, they stop taking the test.

Since they use it daily within their own writing, this doesn't take as long as you might think. As students' spelling test grades rise and hopefully demonstrate a satisfactory level of daily competence, you can then take other spelling words from their daily written work and form future spelling lists around these new words.

Choice 2 Simply take the 70 words and put them up on giant chart paper or on a bulletin board. Offering it as a permanent spelling list of common words that are expected to be spelled properly is quite clear and non-threatening.

Choice 3 New vocabulary words chosen weekly by the students, taken directly from their literature, can be listed on a word wall. Once a week, a combined vocabulary, definition, and spelling test can be given. We've experimented, successfully, giving this as a take-home test between parent and child. This reduces the workload in school.

If this is taken with the expectation that the frequently misspelled words must be spelled correctly, then it would be a useful way to incorporate vocabulary into a spelling test.

We've combined Choice 2 and Choice 3 and experienced student success as well as parent enthusiasm and support.

How Do I Begin?

You're excited. "Pictures" is developmental and goes by successive levels as you progress. LEVEL ONE is where you and your class will start.

Chapter 1, immediately following, will directly address the question of how to begin on your first day, and more.

CHAPTER 1

Section One

Level One—First Day

```
PICTURES—4 sentences = 1 paragraph
```

Here are some typical examples of what you might see on the first day.

G Christina B.

9/11/96

We were playing volleyball in the sun at the beach. My hands were in position to bump and legs were bent, on the sand. I was thinking of were to bump the volleyball. I bumped the volleyball.

Christina

Natasha was dancing to music. My hands were going back and forth, my feet were doing the roll. I thouth I was the bomb. Then I kept dancing and dancing.

Natasha

1st sentence—WHAT IS THE PICTURE?

This sentence should explain what the student-drawn illustration is about.

2nd sentence—SHOW NOT TELL ("SNT")

HANDS and FEET (first level)

This sentence should tell what the hands are doing and the feet are doing, separately from each other.

3rd sentence—THOUGHTS

What is the character in the illustration thinking?

4th sentence—NEXT EXACT MOVEMENT

What Do I Say and Do?

Here is a general idea of what we say and do on our first day. Feel free to change and/or adapt it to suit your own personality.

> "Class, I'd like to introduce you to a writing exercise that is called 'WRITING PICTURES.' I understand that many of you are hesitant about writing.
>
> "This exercise requires you to quickly sketch, within a few minutes, one moment from your daily life. It should be something simple such as eating breakfast, waiting at the bus stop, waking up in the morning, or simply reading a book. It is your choice, but must be real. Remember . . . I am looking for one moment in your life.
>
> "You will be writing four structured sentences each day. We will go through the format together, and each sentence will be thoroughly explained and clarified."

Because our students are living in a technological world that is dominated by television, we have found that many of them are unaccustomed to visualizing a thought. Quick dramatizations help to clarify their thoughts.

Quick Dramatizations

First sentence.   Ask a student to freeze while pretending to read a book. We ask the class to tell us what is the picture at that point.

We rephrase each answer so that it forms a sentence.

The whole class decides on one sentence that it feels best answers the question of "What is the picture?" It is written on the board and properly indented.

> i.e.   <u>The boy sat at his desk reading a book.</u>

Second sentence.   Focus their attention on the hands and feet of the student model. We ask them to tell us separately what the hands and feet are doing. Again, we rephrase what they say, making sure that it stays within one sentence.

We choose their best example and place it after the first sentence so that a paragraph begins to emerge.

> i.e.   The boy sat at his desk reading a book. <u>His hands turned the page and his feet were resting on the floor.</u>

Third sentence.   Ask the student model to tell us what he/she is thinking. It is common for the student model to say, "I don't know." Reassure the student model that any answer is acceptable. Sit back and WAIT. Once the student understands that you are quite comfortable waiting for him/her to gather his/her thoughts together, he/she will manage to think of something.

Once he/she tells you what he/she is thinking, rephrase it to form a complete sentence. Place that sentence immediately after the second sentence.

> i.e.   The boy sat at his desk reading a book. His hands turned the page and his feet were resting on the floor. <u>He was thinking about recess and what he was going to do.</u>

Fourth sentence.   Ask the student model to think of what his/her next movement could be and, at a given signal, to act it out in slow motion. Alert the class to watch the model carefully, paying particular attention to exactly what is happening.

Once again, rephrase the sentence to form a complete sentence and add it to the third sentence. The final result might look something like this.

> i.e.   The boy sat at his desk reading a book. His hands turned the page and his feet were resting

on the floor. He was thinking about recess and what he was going to do. <u>Slowly, he put the book down.</u>

To check understanding, ask another student to freeze while doing something such as eating lunch or making a shot into a basketball hoop. Ask the class to tell you what the first sentence might be. If they do this successfully, ask them for the remaining three sentences. This will tell you immediately whether they have understood the basic format of pictures.

If you feel they need a bit more practice, construct a few more scenarios where students freeze at a certain point of action. Ask students to tell you what the picture is, using the format given previously.

Once the class has demonstrated a fair amount of understanding, you are ready to continue.

Ready to Draw

Have the students turn the page in their black and white composition tablet so that there are two sides—left and right. Explain that on the left side will be the illustrations. The purpose of their illustration is to simply help them visualize what they are writing about. Because of this, their artwork should be quickly sketched within a few minutes, kept extremely simple, and drawn with a pencil only. We call it toothpick art and ask for extensive use of stick figures to keep art time to a minimum. We usually allow only a few minutes for the artwork.

Here are three typical examples of what you might see.

Level One—illustration (a)

Felipe

Level One—illustration (b)

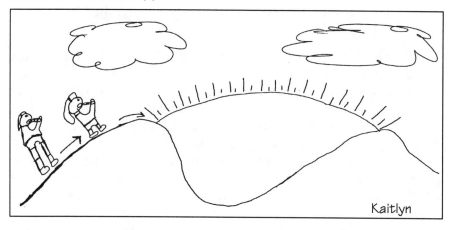

Kaitlyn

Level One—illustration (c)

Jane

If any students are struggling in the actual process of writing the four sentences, encourage them to draw more details. Generally, students who do not have clear details in their writing need more details in their illustration to help them visualize what they are trying to say.

Confident students may very often attempt to begin writing without drawing an illustration. If their writing shows strength, this is fine, since the purpose of illustration is simply to release the beginning writing process, which begins in the mind.

Some students will begin writing first. After looking through what they have written, they will then begin an illustration. This is also fine, since they may be trying to check for details to add to their written work.

Extremely slow students in the upper grades may need flexibility to use colors and time to draw more fully to free their thoughts.

Younger students need to be given more time and the freedom to use crayons and markers because this is part of their writing process. For expediency, you might like to assign the art as homework so that during class they can concentrate on the written aspect.

It is important to remember that the use of illustration in this daily exercise is simply a tool to help clarify the written paragraph.

Ready to Write

On the right side of their tablet, instruct them to write their date and teach them to indent. Upon completion of their illustration, they are to begin writing. Make sure they follow the Level One format previously discussed and practiced. DO NOT HELP TOO MUCH. What you are trying to do is assess their writing abilities. Bite your tongue and stay silent.

Make sure the class understands clearly what to do immediately upon finishing so that it leaves you free to address any concerns that come up. On this first day, we love to schedule some time for easy art, math drill, or silent reading during which all students know exactly what to do.

Using the previous student-drawn illustrations by Felipe, Kaitlyn and Jane, here are their finished attempts from their first day. Notice that they are not polished, have grammatical and/or punctuation errors, have spelling errors, and are repetitious. Don't worry. This is normal.

Level One—pictures (a)

As I was in a play I was so nervouse, My foots was shaking, my hand was numb. My fingers were tired, and I thought I was going to sleep and.

Felipe

Level One—pictures (b)

When my family and I went hiking a couple of months ago, we went to Diamond Head! My hands were moving front and back and my feet were running up the hill. I thought I was going to fall, but I didn't.

Kaitlyn

Level One—pictures (c)

text   9/8/97

This is me eating.

I was by my freind

I was eating with my

hands, my feet was

Moveing. my Body was

moveing,

Jane

What Does the Teacher Do?

As the students work on their four sentences, walk around. On a note pad, jot notes about skills that you notice are missing. We are fully aware that their writing, especially on this first day, may reflect many concerns. If we tried to jot notes about all the skills that are lacking, we would take many hours in this first effort. Think of it this way: you have one entire school year to work at the skills they are missing.

Understanding this, keep your notes to a minimum and confine them to the most obvious problems. Some of these may be a lack of understanding of the format, and perhaps missing dates, not beginning with capitals, and not matching illustrations with the text.

By the time the last student is finished, you will have at least a beginning idea of what their writing abilities are. Remember—students write only four sentences, which makes it easy for the teacher to quickly assess their writing.

There is a temptation to take all the tablets and write comments about the skills that you see lacking. Resist this tendency. This first day should be reserved for simple assessment and kept friendly and safe.

Here are four more examples of what you might see on the first day. Notice the broad range of abilities and errors. All these errors are absolutely normal.

> When the boy throws the yo-yo down, it spins at the bottom of the string. He is standing straght and tall while holding the yo-yo off the ground. He is thinking about doing "walk the dog." But then he decides not to and palls it up.
>
> Jake

> During the movie, Stephanie got up and started heading toward the girl's bathroom in a hurry. Her hands were quiet and her feet quickly tiptoed in the direction of the bathroom. She thought, "How much longer can I hold it?" Stephanie quietly went.
>
> Christina

Level 1

While jumping up and down, the girl said see the bird flying and flat happy. Her hands are going aorund anda her are jumping. She is thinking can she go fast. Her hands begain going faster and faster.

Sheena

I'm doing the papers, and I am getting ready turn around to the next house. I'm doing the papears, and my feet are pedaling the bike. I thought I had thrown it on the porch but it was on the sidewalk. So I took it up and threw it on the porch, Then I pedaled home.

Fluke

In younger grades, we would suggest doing pictures as a class for a minimum of two weeks, and, if needed, for one month to lay the foundation. One picture could be drawn on the board, perhaps drawn by a child, and the entire class could then collaborate to decide what the four sentences should be. If done for one month, the foundation should be set and the children should then be able to work independently with a clearer understanding of what is expected.

End of the Day

Hooray! It is the end of the first day. Spend a few minutes relaxing, grab a cup of something to drink, something to nibble on, and take a look at the notes that you've written earlier in the day. Reflect back on what you noticed regarding the clarity of understanding by the class. Look closely at whether you need to reteach or dramatize again. Check to see if there are any problems with movement, such as where to place the tablets when done and what to do after they are completed.

The following days will be a simple reteaching and reinforcing of everything you have done on the first day. It gets easier with time and practice.

Most teachers at this point begin to wonder, "What do I do next?" Don't worry. Section Two will take you carefully through the next day, first week and address all your concerns that deal with what to do next.

Section Two

Level One—First Week

By the end of the first week, you will see a wide variety and range of abilities in each four sentence paragraph. Remember, the format stays the same.

Be Consistent

During this first week, the students should learn that from now on, they are to quickly sketch and write about a different moment from their own life each day, and that pictures will always be at a certain time of the day, every single day. They should understand that, like writers, they need to write daily, rarely skipping a day, thereby establishing a daily routine.

"Think about what you could write, and always look for a picture in your daily lives" should be the teachers' cry as students leave for the day.

What Does the Teacher Do?

Each day, during this first week, the teacher should review the basic format with the class so that it becomes automatic. Daily mini-lessons during this week should be short, 5–10 minutes in length, and confined to basic review and reminders.

Reminders should also be given that illustrations should be kept simple and to the point; stick figures, quickly drawn, taking only a few minutes, work fine.

Let the students become comfortable with this basic format. Do not be distressed by the many mistakes that you find, nor by the quality of writing that you see. Remember, you have the entire school year to teach the necessary skills. Good writing takes time.

Looking Over Daily Tablets

As the students work, feel free to comment upon one or two concerns, such as a lack of periods or capital letters, that you notice and ask them to correct their errors. Draw their attention to the spelling board if you have one, or a spelling list chart. Clearly show them that spelling does count.

This shows the students what you are focusing on and what they should actively, and on a daily basis, be trying to correct and remember as they write.

By doing this, you are demonstrating clearly that, although you honor and welcome their individual written ideas, they need to pay attention to the mechanics of writing as well. You are also finding out whether they understood your mini-lesson, what skills are lacking, what new concerns are emerging, and most important, how your students are progressing as writers.

Choice 1   Perhaps the easiest way to look at these tablets daily is to peek over the students' shoulders as they write and ask them to make minor corrections immediately. Make sure to focus on only a few concerns. If you bog yourself down in a large variety of punctuation, spelling and grammatical problems, you will take an extremely large chunk of time out of your school day. This will, in turn, make the daily exercise of pictures become laborious.

Choice 2   Another method is to simply wait until the tablets are completed. If you accept the student's tablet, it will indicate that he/she is done and can move on to the next activity. If you do not accept the tablet, it indicates there is a minor problem that you want him/her to focus and work on right at that moment.

Choice 3   Another way is to simply collect all tablets so that you can look at them carefully at a quiet time.

It is important to remember that you should not cover their written work with many red marks, or whatever color you choose to use. Think of yourself. Would you want to correct something that had many corrections indicated? Probably not.

Remember: On an everyday basis, limit yourself to only one or two corrections that you've discussed in mini-lessons or major problems that should be dealt with immediately. Look at the next two examples.

I was swimming at the swimming pool. My leg were going up and down, and my arms were going back and forward. I thought this is fun.

4th sentence is missing.

Jennifer

Text
date
I was talking to my freind while goning up the stairs. We were holding on to the railing and walking up. When where we goning to class, He looked back.

indent

good description

Aaron

Although there are several different types of errors that seem to need attention, notice how we have kept our corrections to a minimum.

Choice 4   Sometimes, looking over the tablets daily becomes cumbersome, despite your best efforts. You may want to have the students self-check their own work, have the checking done by partners, or simply check the tablets on an alternate basis, every other day.

Yet another possibility is to do only one solid sentence each day, out of the total four sentences. For instance, you could work on sentence number one, the topic sentence, for one entire week. This makes it easy to check and spot any possible problems with a minimum of time being spent.

If you choose to look over these tablets at your leisure, we have found reading these paragraphs to be a pleasurable and eye-opening experience, since we now are faced with a very manageable four sentences as well as a structured format.

As the students begin to understand the basic format, daily schedule, and revision/editing corrections, remember to stress that the first sentence should always match their illustration.

If you are still having concerns in this area, go back to dramatization. We have found that dramatizing quickly lightens the classroom and clarifies problem areas immediately.

On the second or third day, the students may begin having problems with proper "tense." Do a review of "tense" with various words, being sure to include tricky tense for words such as *think, eat, sit, bring,* and *swim.* A worksheet, as in Appendix D, or exercises from a Language Arts textbook or workbook can be done.

By now, you're thinking of grades and accountability. You feel fairly comfortable with the four sentences, you have a general idea of the abilities of the students and some weaknesses that you need to explore, and you are wondering about TESTS.

Tests

We give tests once a week. This serves the purpose of keeping each student focused, accountable, and able to measure their progress.

If you are fairly confident that each student is well aware of what the four sentences should be, and is trying to remember to indent and write the date daily, he/she is ready for a test.

Skill Folder

In preparation for this weekly test, each student should have a skill folder that has been clearly labeled with their name, along with a corresponding number. On the next page, you will see two samples of two separate skill folders from which you can choose.

Sample skill folder (a)—Choice 1; Alphabet Chart, Skill List

Sample skill folder (b)—Choice 2; Skill List (blank), Skill List

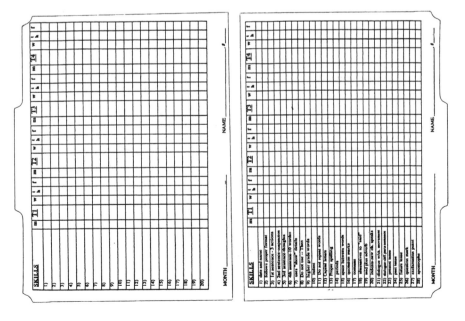

This skill folder will reflect weekly test grades, as well as any grammatical concerns and/or skills that need to be reinforced throughout the following week in preparation for the next weekly test. This skill folder can also reflect spelling concerns as they crop up on an individualized basis. As students' tests accumulate, their skills listed in the folder will also grow. We will address this more clearly in the next few paragraphs.

First Week—First Test (written on folder paper)

30-minute time frame.

You are ready to begin. You have chosen Friday as your test day. Any day will do. Although we have indicated a 30-minute time frame, please feel free to be flexible with the time allotted.

Note: This test can also be given as homework. Parent help is encouraged, since discussion between parent and child can only help. We have experimented with this and received enthusiastic parent feedback. Since the format is so structured, short, and simple, parents feel confident about how to help their child.

No mini-lesson will be presented today. A simple review and a reminder of basic format and housekeeping procedures are enough.

You should still gently remind students who tend to draw too long that they need to be more aware of the time frame given.

Make sure students who are done with their test know what to do next, such as reading silently or working on a previously assigned ongoing project, so that there is a smooth transition between students who are still working on tests and students who are done.

We make sure that our favorite marking pen is ready, along with a red marking pen that we use to circle the final given grade.

We also make sure to have on hand a post-it note pad (recipe card size), so that potential mini-lesson ideas derived from the corrected tests can be jotted down. It is from these notations that mini-lessons are put together for the following weeks.

Correcting the Tests

The first thing to do is to go through the entire four sentences first with a colored marking pen. Mark everything.

Correct all incorrect spelling words by writing the proper spelling above each word. Expect the students to attend to these. We have them write each misspelled word 5 times and keep a spelling chart.

Circle the date if it's missing and correct all improper tense usage and any mechanical problems such as periods and capital letters. Here is an example of a first week test and how it was corrected.

Skill folder (sample a)   Once a tablet has been completely corrected to our satisfaction, we open the skill folder and, on the right side, write "TEST," still using colored pen, where it says genre, the date, and choose and list one or two of the most pressing problems that we feel need to be looked at and reinforced on a daily basis. In the case above, here is what we would have done.

date	genre	skill
9/3/98	TEST	don't forget date, indent

You will soon notice that some students have quite a few skills that need to be pointed out. Some students have very few. Some have none at all. This is normal.

The intent of the column marked "skill" is for the teacher to write individualized skill concerns, taken from students' tests once a week.

Purpose and intent of the skill folder   During the days and weeks immediately following the test, and from then on, there will be certain expectations. It will be expected that individual students look at their skill folders DAILY. It will also be expected, upon completion of their daily pictures writing requirement, that each student will check and make sure that he/she has paid attention to all skills notated in his/her skill folder.

This daily reinforcement helps students focus on grammar and punctuation concerns that you might have discussed during class. They also learn to self-edit and revise by having a handy individualized list to look through that points out exactly which skills they are expected to know and apply thus far.

It is perfectly fine to have no skills under the skill column, next to the column marked "TEST," if it is not merited. Eventually, as mini-lessons continue to be taught and the students develop and stretch their writing, skills needing to be reinforced will surface on their tests.

We make sure to keep the skills that we notate simple, kid-friendly, and written in language that any student and/or parent would be able to interpret and understand. Remember, if students cannot make sense of what has been written, they will not be able to apply it in their daily writing.

When we are done making corrections and notating the skills in their skill folder that we want the students to reinforce in their daily writing, we write their test grade and circle it.

date	genre	skill
9/3/98	TEST (B+)	don't forget date, indent

Spelling?

You are probably wondering what happened to the spelling words that we corrected for the students directly on their tests using a marker. If you look at the left side of the skill folder, you will notice an alphabetized three-column chart (see Appendix E). The first page has A, B, C, and the pages that follow contain three letters of the alphabet on each page.

We teach the students to understand that upon taking this test, each of us has a job to do. Our job is to peruse their written work upon completion, to notate skills we feel are lacking, to correct improperly spelled words, and to grade the tests.

Their job is to look over their tests prior to turning them in, reflect upon their mistakes, and make changes accordingly. When the tests are returned, they are expected to attend to all grammatical, punctuation, and spelling corrections indicated.

Spelling Choices

Choice 1 Have them rewrite all spelling words that have been marked accurately and alphabetically in their chart for future reference.

Choice 2 Have them write each misspelled word five or ten times on the back.

Choice 3 Have them rewrite the test in its entirety, corrected accurately, so that they practice writing a proper paragraph with proper punctuation and spelling. *We like this one!*

Through sheer daily use and the continuous expectation of proper spelling and use of their chart, their spelling begins to improve.

Second Test—Second Week

Although we are technically still in the first week in accordance with this section, we would like to state that all tests from the second week on would be administered in exactly the same way.

Let's review

First, establish a day and time for your pictures test. Upon completion of what the students feel is their best effort, they are to check their skill folder prior to turning it in. This will be expected daily from here on, including the day of the test.

Once the first test has been given, this should become a familiar routine—a simple, but expected extra step. Let us repeat: Students should check their skill folder every single day upon completion of their pictures paragraph, and make appropriate corrections from the notes the teacher has written from the test of the previous week.

As you receive these tests, do the same thing you did in the first test. Correct all spelling words, make all corrections and begin notating a few of them on the skill folder.

If you notice that certain skills from the previous week have not been applied, simply put a *red marker dot* next to those skills to alert the students upon receiving them that they have not paid attention to those skills. Of course, the students should understand that this will result in a lower grade, since it is expected that they will pay attention to the skills marked. In this way, we can make sure that grammar and spelling issues are being attended to, and that their knowledge of these skills and their applications continue to grow. It should look something like this.

date	genre	skill
9/3/98	TEST (B+)	don't forget date indent *
9/10/98	TEST (B)	check skill list capitalize letters that begin sentence

    With time, patience and practice, you will grow more comfortable with this procedure.

Skill folder (sample b)   This skill folder, *which we prefer,* emphasizes individual student goal setting. This helps students be more aware of what they should be looking for before they turn their written paragraph in.

   Right side

   On one side, you will see a skill chart, numbered 1 through 28, with a wide variety of skills that we will be trying to address throughout the school year.
   On the top, you will see **m, T1, w, th, f.** This indicates the days of the week, and is repeated four times, equaling one month. Each **T1, T2, T3,** and **T4,** reflects a Tuesday and the day that a test grade will be given. We have chosen Tuesday as our test day, however, it should be made clear that any day chosen is completely at the discretion and scheduling of the teacher.

Daily

Students are to exchange their written paragraphs and skill folders with their partners and check off each other's goals. The teacher should not look at these daily check marks, since we are trying to teach students to be responsible and self-conference for themselves. We know the temptation is great to red mark and critically pick up on all mistakes. Resist this temptation. Confine yourself to looking at these tablets visually, without a pen in hand.

For a review of choices on how to look over these tablets on a daily basis, look back at pages 12–14.

Sometime during the first month that Level One is taught, all students should become aware of the requirements to complete numbers 1 through 15 accurately.

Feel free to alter the skills marked as needed to reflect grade level differences or individual backgrounds of the students. An example of this might be to ask for only one action detail in the first sentence. Another example might be to ask for only 5 words in the fourth sentence. As the students progress, you can choose to bring the original marked skill back.

On a daily basis, before students indicate they are completed, they should put a check mark next to the corresponding column and under the appropriate day, to accurately reflect that they have attended to these skills.

During the school year, the teacher should then expand their goal setting from numbers 1 through 15 to extend to the other numbers as each new skill is introduced.

Test Day

Once the test is completed, make all necessary corrections. Spelling, punctuation, grammar, content, format—anything goes.

As you correct these tests, put a red minus sign, in the appropriate column, either **T1, T2, T3,** or **T4,** and in the corresponding numbered space where you feel a skill is missing or has not been attended to. You may also notice that you are looking for skills not listed on this chart. They may be simple, such as subject verb agreement or the use of transition words. There may also be issues such as the checking off of the skill chart on a daily basis, or housekeeping issues such as where to put the tablets when they are completed that you want to emphasize.

These skills may be indicative of a lesson you taught and now want the entire class to attend to from now on. They may, however, represent only the particular needs of certain individual students.

You may feel the urge to write this somewhere for students to closely focus on from now on.

Left side.

On the other side of this folder, you will see the exact same skill chart, this time without the skills typed in. Remember to mark the skill chart, both left and right side, only on test day. It is on this blank skill chart that you as the teacher may write any other skills or concerns that you want emphasized.

After you write them in, remind students that any red minuses indicated on either or both skill charts should now be attended to on a daily basis.

Explain that some students will have many skills written in by the teacher and some students may have a minimal amount or none. Explain that you are helping them as a class, and individually, so that they may continue to grow as writers.

Don't worry if students are neither attending nor being responsible on a daily basis for the skill chart. Once a week on "test day," you will be able to see whether they have been checking off their skills on a daily and responsible basis. At this time, write "check your skill chart on both sides daily," and add this on to the skill chart. You may also choose this issue as a mini-lesson for future reference.

About Spelling

Go back to page 18 and 19 and look at choices 2 and 3. We like to do a combination of these because then the students will have the chance to write their corrected test accurately, see what it should look like, and spell each word ten times.

About Grading

We never grade below a C– because we understand that writing is threatening to most students. We want to establish a safe environment where writing is encouraged and kept positive.

The issue of subjective grading is also threatening to many teachers, ourselves included.

We remember worrying about what grade to give and how to justify it to students and parents. A grade was given that was thought to be in the right vicinity and we generally prayed it would be okay. Not very professional, admittedly, but the only way we could survive.

We began grading students together with other teachers. We discussed issues of fairness, rubrics, subjectivity, writing concerns, and anything else we could think of. We brought our students into our discussions and, finally, invited them into our concerns about grading.

We finally agreed that the exact following of the format, nothing more, nothing less, would be graded in the range of a C. Look at the example on page 17 that Sheena wrote for her first week test. You can see that her test falls under the guidelines of following the format. She does not have a strong command of language and has numerous mistakes that need to be looked at. We can then say that her test might be given a grade of C.

If students exhibit more skill, however, by paying attention to grammar and spelling concerns, as well as trying to use better vocabulary, then their effort would result in a grade in the range of a B.

> I'm double checking my school supplies because school is two days away. One hand is checking things off on the list my other is counting different things and my feet are scuffing the floor. I'm thinking "Boy, I have a lot of stuff. Suddenly one of my pink pencils dropped on the floor.
>
> Whitney

> On a bright early morning, I was running really hard, trying to catch up with friends because we were badly late for school. My hands were like frozen ice and my feet were running as if bees were chasing me. I was thinking I would be grounded when I get home.
>
> Jonathan

Writing that demonstrated beauty, higher-level vocabulary, attention to revision and editing concerns, and attention to detail would result in a grade in the range of an A.

Scrambling over the fence to get away from the vicious dog, I accidently got my pants stuck to his teeth and tried to escape. My fingers grasped the fence and my foot tried to strike the dog. "I'm going to die," I mumbled, I managed to get over the fence and stuck my tongue at the dog.

Felipe

Once we could agree on a general comfort zone of grades, we began to feel more confident about issuing grades as well as explaining why those grades were given. We welcomed student input and used their comments about each other's work to clarify what grades were merited so that we were all comfortable. The students were able to transfer their knowledge of why they received those grades and tried to push themselves toward a higher grade in the following weeks.

We noticed a curious thing begin to happen. When the students knew exactly what formula to follow, and had a fair idea of how their grades were derived, they began to pay closer attention to their writing.

Our classes became filled with intense concentration. They self-edited and self-revised as they checked with their own skill folders to make sure attention had been paid to these concerns and exhibited an overall eagerness to reach for a higher level of writing.

Fearful?

The correction of these tests, once a week, may seem like a monumentally large task. Don't worry. We can assure you, from first-hand experience, that it quickly gets easier as you get into a rhythm and routine.

What's Next?

Now that you've successfully completed your first full week, reflect back on what you've accomplished and smile. Although clumsy, your students are learning the format of pictures and your daily procedures.

You are now ready to continue full steam ahead with Level One. This level may take approximately one month, give or take individual class differences. During this month, you will be emphasizing and exploring new vocabulary, laying a firm foundation, dramatizing, discovering the joy of sharing with each other, and growing as a writer.

Remember that Level One follows the same format every single day. It is not your job to think of new ideas to write about. That job belongs to your students.

Section Three

Level One—First Month

By the end of the month, you will see a wide range of abilities. Most students will understand clearly what to do and will surprise you with the range and growth of their writing.

> The man was driving a huge monster truck along a dirt road. His feet were resting on the gas pedal and he was holding on to the steering wheel. He was thinking about how much fun it was going to be to run over the cars. But then the engine broke down so he got out and fixed it.
>
> Jake

> One day, a little green caterpillar was eating on a fresh, dark green leaf that came from a willow tree. He twitched his antennae's and wiggled his toes. He thought, "Oh, what a day!" But then a dark shadow appeared and he turned around and there he saw a hungry bird so he jumped into a hole in the tree.
>
> Jessica

Sprinting down the drenched hill, I ran as fast as I could to catch the bus. My hands were clenched into balls and I looked down and felt a whipping on my leg. I thought my shoelaces were untied. When I stopped to tie them, the bus passed by and I had to walk to school.

Fluke

Let's Review

All students should have, as their automatic daily homework assignment, a moment in their life prepared in their mind prior to actually beginning. The chosen moment should be kept simple. Waiting in the car, licking an ice cream cone, doing homework in your room with the radio on full blast, waiting in the grocery line, or simply watching television are all possibilities. The choices are endless.

The illustration is not the final purpose, the text is. As a result, the actual illustration should take only a few minutes. Lower grades will, of course, take quite a bit longer since this is part of their writing process.

The students should also clearly understand that your minor corrections are to help them become aware of the quality and level of their writing. At the same time, it will be easy to see whether they are paying even half-hearted attention to their skill folders, prior to turning them in.

Remember, your marking of every single correction on their paper should be reserved for test day only. If you feel the need to correct them daily, keep your corrections simple and brief.

Remember the first test? From that test on, every day, test or no test, skill folders should be looked at as the students write. Upon completion of what they feel is their final product, they should then check any revision and/or editing that has been indicated by the previous week's test.

From the second week on, throughout the remaining levels, it is important to remember that a short mini-lesson should always be taught daily. Don't panic!

Mini-lessons can be as simple as reminding students to write their date and/or to indent at the beginning of their paragraph.

New mini-lessons can be based upon grammar or punctuation concerns that you notice.

A good rule of thumb is to present two or three NEW mini-lessons within one week. The mini-lessons on remaining days can be simple reminders.

Mini-Lessons

Each day, reinforce the proper format of pictures. During this first month of Level One, you will probably teach several types of mini-lessons more than once. Here are the most common.

1. *Past, present, and future tense.* Give them a teacher-made worksheet, Appendix D, or simply use a language exercise from a textbook or workbook. We like to have them work in groups so that a healthy discussion about proper placement of tense ensues. Take this extra time to make sure this is understood since this seems to be one of the biggest problems of young writers, at least editorially.

2. *Three details or actions in the first sentence.* Since the first sentence is the main topic sentence, we want to make sure it is rich in detail and flows with good vocabulary. Drama, looking through literature, and providing words, Appendix G, will help your students stretch themselves and open a window into the use of wonderful words to help make meaning richer.

   Example.

   We have a predrawn picture of a young girl eating her breakfast cereal in the kitchen with her dog beside her chair. There is a fishbowl in the far corner of the room and her mother is at the sink washing dishes. The sunlight is streaming in and the scene looks cozy and warm.

   If the students have initial difficulty moving past the sentence, *"The girl is eating cereal,"* we prompt them by asking questions such as where is she, is there anyone by her, and what is she sitting on.

   With much encouragement, prompting and discussion, they move from the simple *"The girl is eating cereal,"* to the more detailed and complex, *"The girl is eating cereal in the kitchen with her dog by her chair."* Even in this simple sentence, differences and some maturity can be seen emerging.

3. *1st sentence—beginnings.* Discuss sentence beginnings and caution them about overusing "I." Probably one of the biggest problems we've run across has been the famous "I," "then," or "and." The students get remarkably inventive using "and then," "so then," "but then," "now then," and even try "As I," "When I," "And I," and "Soon I." The list is endless. To solve this problem, we've banned all use of the word "then" and limited the use of the word "I."

    As the students grow comfortable with the basic format of pictures, we notice a fairly exclusive use of the same type of nouns beginning to emerge, especially in the first sentence. Do these sound familiar? "My friends and I . . .", "My dad and I . . .", "My dog . . .", "As I . . .", "The boy . . .", "The teacher . . .". The list goes on.

    To combat this, we open discussions about different ways to begin. We search through literature and discuss beginning through characterization, description of a setting, an action, and/or dialogue. We solicit examples from the students' own writings, and ask them to look through literature for examples from published authors. We go back to the use of drama to help us better visualize the picture.

    We have found that a verb or action phrase is a wonderful way to begin. Our students quickly enjoy acting out the many offered suggestions, such as trembling with fear, slashing the air, leaning over the rail, eating in the cafeteria, and other similar ideas.

    To further demonstrate this, we use the same picture above of the girl eating cereal, asking them to remember to include at least three details and to begin with a verb or action phrase. With their drama practice, the class can now progress to something like this:

    > *"Munching her cereal, the girl sat in her chair, watching her mother move around in her breakfast way."*

You will notice that by bringing closer attention to the use of verb or action phrases, and coupling that with the requirement of including three details or actions, the first sentence now dramatically changes. The sentence becomes more detailed and interesting. They are now paying closer attention to the more minute details of their picture.

Students who still experience some difficulty should be gently encouraged to include a bit more detail in their illustration before writing. Their lack of details in their written work might be the result of a lack of details in their illustration. With daily practice, most of the students will be strengthening their visualization skills. With time, you will notice less and less drawing is necessary for some of your more capable students.

4. *2nd sentence—use of hands and feet.*   In the second sentence, you may notice that the use of "hands and feet" is getting tiresome, redundant, and even awkward. Once students are comfortable with the idea that they need to look at both physical features, they should be encouraged to look carefully and make fine distinctions between when to use "my hands" and when to use "I."

    For example, think about the sentence *"My hands were holding the pencil"* and compare it to *"I held the pencil."* It is quite obvious which is better. Yet, look closer at this sentence: *"My hands were frozen blocks of ice."* Upon closer inspection, it becomes clear that if the hands are in motion, you would then use *"I."* If, however, hands are the object, you would then need to keep it as *"My hands."* This takes time and practice, but don't be discouraged when your students have difficulty. Keep trying and your patience will bear fruit.

5. *3rd sentence—I don't know.*   Probably the easiest of all sentences is the third sentence. "I'm not thinking of anything" or "I don't know" should never be accepted. Encourage them to explore, through drawing if necessary, what they might be thinking at that time. Ask them to think deeper and delve inside of themselves so that they can begin to explore the early stages of character development.

Some students write "I was thinking" and "I thought." Some write "I wonder." Still others write "I can imagine." At this stage, it really doesn't matter. As individual students exhibit a need, teach quotation marks to them and move on.

6. *4th sentence—transition.*   This sentence helps the writer to move into beginning a new paragraph. It should focus on what exact movement happened next. This helps the students to clarify the picture even more and, furthermore, helps the reader make the transition toward the next sequence of events.

   If this is difficult, continue emphasizing dramatization. Ask individual volunteer students to act out a picture and freeze. Ask the volunteer to slowly act out their next movement and ask the class to guess what the next movement might be. With enough modeling and time, this becomes much easier for them.

7. *Exploring a second paragraph.*   At some point within this first month, LEVEL ONE, you will notice that some students can finish quite easily within the half an hour allotted, given 5–10 minutes for a mini-lesson and the remaining time to draw and write.

   These students can be encouraged to draw another picture BELOW THE FIRST ILLUSTRATION, and begin their next written paragraph BELOW THE FIRST WRITTEN PARAGRAPH, following the same original format. Be sure students clearly understand that their second paragraph should still follow the original four sentence format.

   This second picture, second paragraph, will take time, since the first hurdle you will encounter will be confusion as to what to do in the new paragraph. Don't worry. This is to be expected.

   Explain to your students that this second paragraph will take time and patience. With practice, their second paragraph will improve.

   Initially, we would not include these second paragraphs in their weekly test grade. By Level Three, however, we would definitely consider including it as a way to "nudge" them into longer writing.

8. *Connection to Literature.*   When students are struggling to "grow" their sentences, perhaps the easiest way is to help them by searching through literature. It is not uncommon for us to spend one entire week not doing pictures. We spend the time searching through literature for good topic sentences that show details and write them in our writers journal. Another way is to take these sentences and write them on chart paper, to which the class can add other sentences throughout the week. In this way, sentences that show detail are clearly emphasized in a non-threatening manner. In the following week, we then go back to our pictures format, emphasizing the need to look carefully for details as we have done during the previous week.

9. *Time.*   The length of time each teacher spends on pictures is a personal choice. Remember, pictures is usually thirty minutes a day. Because we spend so much time with literature connections, and grammar and spelling concerns, one month per level is quite normal for us. If needed, we do not hesitate to take longer.

Ending Thoughts

You have ended Level One and if you're anything like us, you are filled with a good feeling. Your students are comfortable with the daily routine of pictures and are beginning to show individual writing styles. Their writing is beginning to bloom and you are probably deriving pleasure from reading their individual efforts.

Section Four

Review

Now that approximately one month has elapsed, students and teachers are fairly comfortable with the process of pictures. Keep in mind that you should continuously review with your students the format so that it is clear.

It should be understood that mini-lessons will be given daily, and that grammar, punctuation and spelling will be taught and expected to be used within the context of their daily written pictures.

It should also be clearly understood that tests or quizzes will be given once weekly, that they should understand how the skill folder works, become accustomed to mini-lessons, and most important, come to school prepared to write.

Why Don't I See Remarkable Results?

Even with all this daily practice and clarity, you might still feel that the written work of your students is "clone-like." Be patient! You will see growth and individual differences begin to emerge.

To get a wonderful product, process is everything. If something is attempted once a week or once every so often, the results will be mimimal.

Think of the metaphor of a house. The process of writing pictures can be compared to the building of a house. Without a solidly built foundation based upon high expectations and time given, the results will be, at best, decent. Students will understand how to write a basic paragraph, complete with topic sentence and supporting details. This would be a house with only a frame, no furnishings or architectural details.

If students are to produce higher-level vocabulary, fluidity of style, grace of expression, and power, they need to have consistent, daily practice.

Writing exercises are neither glamorous nor exciting. It would be easy to think or to say that it is boring, repetitive, and nonproductive. Indeed, there might be days when it would be hard to think otherwise.

"What's the point of writing the same thing every day?"

"My students don't change."

"They don't come to school prepared to write!"

"I don't see tremendous improvement."

"It's the same old thing."

"It sounds clumsy and repetitious to me."

You must be patient. Good writing takes time to develop and grow.

Think about a recipe. Before you can experiment and make something uniquely your own, you need to learn from an actual recipe and try it many times first.

Think about basketball. Before you can work on your own individual moves, or create something fancy, you need to work at basic skills such as dribbling, passing and shooting.

Think about piano music. Before you can compose your own music, you need to practice scales, learn theory, gain knowledge of the notes, and understand the basic composition of music.

The same concept applies to our approach to writing.

With each progressive Level, and as time is given daily, as persistence is exercised by you and your students, and as you are buoyed up by your own high expectations, you will begin to see differences. Students will feel more confident, pay more attention to the use of spelling, grammar and punctuation, and most important, begin to show their individual differences in styles of writing.

CHAPTER 2

Level Two

Playing excitedly with my dad, I surprisingly threw the ball over his head and he was amazed by what I did. My dad asked, "how did you do that?" I just said, "I extended my arm and threw the ball with all my strength." I thought when I threw it, it was going to land short. Later, when we struggled to get back to the car, I asked my dad if we could go to McDonald's.

Fluke

In the morning, I woke up with my head as hot as an iron. I was so sick I had to push myself off my bed, landing on my feet. I thought if I kept on coughing everyone would catch my dizziness and sickness. When I stopped coughing, everyone came running in the room coughing and pointing at me.

Jason

1st sentence—WHAT IS THE PICTURE?

include three details

begin with a verb or action phrase

2nd sentence—SHOW NOT TELL ("SNT")

hands or feet (choose one or the other)

one sense (choose from the five senses)

3rd sentence—THOUGHTS

4th sentence—EXACT NEXT MOVEMENT

In this level, notice that only the second sentence changes. Everything else stays the same.

How Do I Begin?

Give yourself about one hour, since today will be the beginning of a new level and you want to make sure you have enough time to leisurely go through it. Although it is not hard, you still want the comfort of having plenty of time.

Each time you begin a new level, allot about a one-hour time period. You may not need all that time, but it's nice to have it.

Begin with a basic review as usual. This will help keep the students in familiar territory and will reinforce the idea that the basic format of pictures will always stay the same, with minor adjustments to differentiate between each level.

Upon completion of the review, begin your introduction into the new adjustment. Draw their attention to the second sentence and point out that it is the only sentence that has changed. All other sentences stay the same. This should bring about a big sigh of relief from your students.

Quick Reminder: Don't forget that a good rule of thumb for frequency of mini-lessons is two or three NEW mini-lessons per week. The mini-lessons on the remaining days should be confined to quick notes on such things as indenting, paying attention to lack of capital letters, and other such reminders.

Mini-Lesson

Ask your class to remember the quick dramatization sketch that they did on the *first day* of school about the boy reading at his desk. Have it prewritten on the board to refresh their memory.

The boy sat at his desk reading a book. His hands turned the page and his feet were on the floor. He was thinking about recess and what he was going to do. Slowly, he put the book down.

You and the class are probably smiling now and remember this from the first day of pictures.

Quick Dramatization

To help the class better understand the changes that should be happening in their own written work, explain that the previous example of the boy reading a book will be used in a quick dramatization to help clarify Level Two. Ask a student model to take the position of the boy reading a book and whisper to him that in this dramatization he should be tired, and the classroom is muggy. This will help the student model to understand how he should portray the boy reading a book.

Since the students are all familiar with verb or action phrases by now, have them discuss all the possible ways to begin the first sentence differently. Remind them that it must include three details, so they should pay close attention to the details surrounding the boy. Through discussion, the final result of the first sentence might be something like this:

Slouching tiredly over his desk in the muggy classroom, the little boy read his book.

Next, discuss what the five senses are—touch, taste, hear, see, and smell. You might want to post them on the board, especially for younger children. Explain that from now on, they will be moving up to another level of writing and instead of staying with "hands and feet," they should now choose HANDS or FEET and ONE SENSE.

Draw the attention of the class to the hands and feet of the student model and decide what the focus will be. Hands or feet? Once it's decided, ask them to volunteer suggestions as to what the hands or feet are doing. The class-chosen response might be *"His hands were turning the pages."*

Next, ask them to think back to each of the five senses and decide as a class which sense they want to focus on. Remind them that they can only choose one. When they do so, again ask for volunteer suggestions as to how you could incorporate the chosen sense into a sentence. The class-chosen response might be, *"He could feel perspiration dribbling."* If you want to get more details from them, you might ask further, *"Where was the perspiration dribbling?"* to which the class response might be, *"down his back."*

You can either rephrase the sentence and connect it together for them, or ask the students to connect it together so that it forms one complete sentence, linking the hands or feet together with the chosen sense.

With this change, the second sentence of the class might now reflect changes that look like this.

> His hands turned the pages and he could feel perspiration dribbling down his back.

Keeping in mind that the third and fourth sentences do not change at all, the final finished product of the class might look like this:

> Slouching tiredly over his desk in the muggy classroom, the little boy quietly read his book. His hands turned the pages and he could feel perspiration dribbling down his back. He was thinking about recess and what he was going to do. Slowly, he put the book down.

Pretty terrific, don't you think? Your students will be ready to challenge themselves and their writing will reflect this new knowledge.

Second Paragraph

At the same time that you introduce this new level, continue challenging them to write a second paragraph when they are done with the first, but don't belabor this as of yet. The main focus is securing the format within the new second level and encouraging experimentation with their own style.

Further Mini-Lesson Needs

At this point, you will notice some mini-lesson needs that will surface. Here are seven samples.

1. *Thesaurus.*   Students will and should be encouraged to begin bringing in their thesauruses. Mini-lessons should be done on its usage.

2. *Literature.*   Students will and should be encouraged to use their own literature and/or basal textbooks to help them with higher-level vocabulary as well as ideas. We suggest to our students that they put all new words and intriguing language or phrases that they come upon as they read literature, both fiction and non-fiction, into a writer's notebook. This will help them build upon their knowledge of words and give them a place to refer to as the need comes up.

3. *Vocabulary.*   You should probably do some type of vocabulary study at this point. Words can be taken from basal textbooks, workbooks, language textbooks, their daily lives, and anywhere else that has interesting words.

    We usually have weekly vocabulary lists, taken from their literature reading journals. In our class, our students must write responses to literature that they are currently reading. As one part of the requirement, they must include new vocabulary that they come upon. We take these words and discuss them "round table style" on a weekly basis and build up our vocabulary bank in this way.

4. *Notebook.*   A notebook labeled "writer's notebook" can be established, so that students will begin listening for intriguing language, whether its source is their peers, people around them, or literature that they read.

    One day while we were kidding around with the students, one of them decided to tell us something about another student. That student came charging from out of nowhere and yelled out, "Don't go there. You don't want to go there." He had a smile on his face but, from the way he used his humor, we understood immediately that he meant he didn't want that student to say anything personal.

We had never heard that phrase before and enjoyed how it sounded and felt on our tongues. We took delight in using it at opportune moments, especially with the students.

We use this example, then ask for other examples from the students. We discuss the rich language that is used all around us and remind them that as they jot down these bits of language, they can store them as if in a bank and use them in the future as they write.

5. *Using illustrations.*   When they are confused, encourage them to use illustrations to help visualize and clarify what they are trying to say.

6. *Conferencing.*   Encourage discussion, after they write silently, about what they have written. Because the format is so simple, and their skill folder is readily available, they can begin the process of revision and editing quite easily with their peers.

7. *Beginning a second paragraph.*   Beginning a second paragraph, especially for upper grades, can be strongly encouraged. Teach a mini-lesson about sequence of action and storyline so that students stay within the same story instead of jumping to another storyline.

What you don't want is a first paragraph about a boy quietly reading a book, and then the second paragraph suddenly jumping to the boy riding a roller coaster at an amusement park. The students should clearly see that a paragraph about a boy quietly reading a book in class should be followed with that same boy perhaps putting the book away or getting ready for the next subject.

What Does the Teacher Do—Daily?

As in Level One, remember to try to look over each tablet *once daily.* This can be done as you walk around and look over their shoulders. On your always handy post-its, jot down simple notes such as common spelling errors, basic grammar and punctuation concerns, or instances of non-compliance to the format. Keep your notes simple so that your job will be easier.

As discussed in the previous section, save your comprehensive checks for the once-a-week test. Feel free to correct everything and anything. Remember to rewrite all misspelled words for them directly on their paper and attend to editing concerns.

Continue to review basic format daily and add in a mini-lesson according to your class's identified needs. Always remember to begin with a mini-lesson. Remember that a good rule of thumb is to have two or three new mini-lessons per week. The remaining days can be as simple as a basic review, reminders about where to put finished tablets, or what to do next.

Things to Think About

By now, you might notice some students who are able to write well without beginning with an illustration. They show comfort in the process of visualizing their writing in their minds. If their writing is clear, concise, and creates a picture in the reader's mind, using strong language to convey their thoughts, then the illustrative aspect is not as important. However, if the language, sequence, and details of writing are still unformed and at the most basic level, insist that they draw so that they clearly see what images they need to convey.

It would be easy to think that their writing, by this level, should be easy and wonderful to read. Some students will be able to show a great deal of growth with just a little bit of guidance. Most students, however, will continue to struggle along as all writers do. Regardless of ability level, their writing will continue to show more focus and details, as these three young writers do.

As I was at black sand beach I saw turtles. My hands reached for the camera as I took a picture of them and I could feel the sand as it felt like coffee grounds. I thought one of the turtles might pop its head out of the water. Suddenly, it did pop its head out of the water.

Sheena

I'm writing my pictures with a red checkered pencil in my composition tablet which is black and white. I'm doodling all over my paper and glancing at everyone else writing their own paraghraph. I wonder what I'm going to write next because my mind is blankl for ideas. I keep on thinking about what I could write.

Whitney

Playing on the computer, Rochellie and I were cautiously trying to avoid the mouse traps and auxiously figuring what keys to press to make the mouse get the cheese! Rochel. had to quickly move her fingers to make the mouse go in the right direction and I felt my heart beating faster and rapidly in my chest. I thought we were going to go into a mouse trap. I suddenly pressed the wrong key and the mouse went right into the mouse trap.

Sharon

CHAPTER 3

Level Three

Grasping onto my greasy metal pole, my brother and I rode the #49 bus to the beach. My shoulder muscles ached from my heavy backpack and I wanted to plop down just how Jello does when its put on a plate. I pretended the bus had a bomb on it similar to the movie "Speed" with Keanu Reeves. I rolled my eyes clockwise while letting out a grizzly bear type of sigh.

About three seconds after I sighed, a yawn came out of me and I blinked my eyes. My eyes watered and I heard the bell ring for someone to get off. I thought of how to get through the crowd fast enough to the now empty seat. Without hesitation, I ran in the way that a robber does when chased by a policeman.

Christina

As the sun went down and its reflection shimmered in the waveless ocean, the beach was deserted and only occupied by me. A gentle wind blew the sand over my feet and the water and it seemed to blow the sunlight away. "Hi Alison," I called to my friend. As I ran to her, the sun slipped below the horizon.

Whitney

1st sentence—WHAT IS THE PICTURE?

include at least three details begin
with verb or action phrase

2nd sentence—SHOW NOT TELL ("SNT")

<u>one body part</u>
<u>one sense</u>

3rd sentence—THOUGHTS

4th sentence—NEXT EXACT MOVEMENT

In Level Three, the focus is again on the second sentence. We are moving away from the expectation of using hands or feet (although the students are certainly welcome to use them) and are now simply asking for a body part.

Mini-Lesson

As usual, begin with the basic review. This is a very important step since it will always keep the students focused.

On the board, rewrite the paragraph that you used for your Level Two mini-lesson. Remember the one about the boy reading a book?

Have the class read the first sentence and review the components that led to this sentence. They should be able to state that the first sentence should begin with a verb or action phrase and should include three details.

Second sentence—changes

Draw their attention to the second sentence and ask them to choose another body part instead of the hands that they had previously chosen. If this is difficult for them, go back to quick dramatizations and ask a student model to volunteer and act out that moment of reading a book.

Have the class decide together what body part to choose, and have them discuss what is happening to that body part. Some examples might be a leg twitching and getting numb, hair spiked every which way, neck aching, and/or shoulders slumped.

The class's second sentence result might look like this:

> <u>His neck ached and he could feel perspira-</u>
> <u>tion dribbling down his back.</u>

Remind students that the third and fourth sentences do not change at all. Combine the new sentence with the other three familiar ones and the end result should look like this:

> Slouching tiredly over his desk in a muggy classroom, the little boy quietly read his book. <u>His neck ached and he could feel perspiration dribbling down his back.</u> He was thinking about recess and what he was going to do. Slowly, he put the book down.

You will be noticing that the students are becoming more and more comfortable with the daily format of writing, revising, and editing.

Prepositions/Prepositional Phrases

By this time, students may be writing two complete paragraphs. If they are not, don't fret. Keep nudging capable students to complete two paragraphs. Since this only comprises a total of eight sentences, we do not feel it is too much to ask.

Ask students to pay close attention to their first sentence in both paragraphs, making sure it is rich in language and detail.

In the second paragraph, suggest that they begin with a prepositional phrase, Appendix H. We have found that by suggesting choices, the students are forced away from beginning with a noun, and think more carefully about how they can phrase the beginning sentences of their new paragraph.

Draw or dramatize as needed to help clarify movements and actions of characters in the storyline. Keep insisting on three details or actions in the first sentence of each paragraph and expect students to use higher-level vocabulary.

Redundancy

You may begin noticing redundancy at this time, either within one paragraph, or with the addition of a second paragraph. Don't be discouraged. This is a natural occurrence. Our students understand that it is far better to have more words than too few, because it is easier to take out words than it is to add more words.

Here is an example of a student who wrote two paragraphs and was obviously redundant as she struggled to connect the two together.

> Crying my eyes out, I sat at the funeral hall, on a gloomy day. I sat on a cold chair and heard a funeral song begin. I was thinking that I missed him so much. I <u>stood up and walked over to my grandfather's coffin.</u>
>
> <u>As I walked over to my grandfather's coffin, I sobbed.</u> I walked back to my seat and sat down, trying not to begin crying again. "I wish he was alive," I whispered sadly. I told the man to stop playing the funeral song and wept again.
>
> Emily

Draw the students' attention back to how they began their paragraphs. Discuss the issue of redundancy and help them to see where they repeat themselves. Help them to talk through and do further illustrations, if necessary, of the actions of the character. Give them some quiet time and have them try again.

With the help of the teacher, Emily was able to see where her redundancies occurred. She was able to rethink what she was trying to say and restructure her paragraph. Here is her finished product:

> Crying my eyes out on a gloomy day, I sat beside my grandfather's coffin. I sat on a cold chair and heard a funeral song begin. I was thinking that I missed him so much. <u>Slowly, I walked over to my grandfather's coffin.</u>
>
> <u>With no one yet around, I stood there in the eerie quiet and sobbed.</u> I walked back to my seat and sat down, trying not to begin crying again. "I wish he was alive," I whispered sadly. I told the man to stop playing the funeral song and wept again.
>
> Emily

While success will not always be easy, with time and continuous support from the teacher, the students will begin to understand what to avoid and will begin to search for ways to better say what they mean.

Student Samples

To help you better judge how your students are doing, we have included four student samples of this level. You can see the wide range in the abilities of these students.

Creeping slowly towards my mom's seat staring at a roach, I desperately tried to smash it with my wooden stick. My eyes popped out without warning and I saw it crawling closer to Mom's hair. I thought to myself, When am I going to smash that roach? I suddenly yelled out, Mom! There's a roach on your seat!

Cameron

Waking up disturbed because my dad was snoring away, I yawned and stretched my back. I smelled the pancakes and bacon roasting in the hot pan while my mom came and woke up my younger sister, I covered my ears so I wouldn't hear much of the commotion. My brain wished that my dad wouldn't snore so much because then we could get to sleep and be attentive at school. I hustled out of bed quickly and got ready for school.

Sharon

Throwing snowballs at my dad with frost around my face I was ready to dodge his snowballs. My eyes felt like they were going to freeze and I saw a snowball flying straight at me. I thought it would knock me down. The snow ball hit me and I shook my head.

Above the cold snow my face was hurting and I was furious. My arm was reaching for another snowball and I heard my brother come out the front door. I thought I would hit my brother. I threw the snowball at my brother.

Drew

Walking up a hill to my favorite thinking spot under an apple tree, I sat down and started reading. Just then I heard something, I turned my head to look up, and an apple hit me right on the head and knocked me out. When I woke up I thought that a tree branch had hit me. I felt my head to see if I was bleeding, and I felt a big lump, so I got up, walked down the hill to my house, and told my mom what had happend.

Brian

CHAPTER 4

Level Four

Sitting cross-legged on a long narrow bench, I chewed on a stick of gum. My jaw began to tickle as I felt my gum begin to dissolve in my mouth. "Amazing!" I stuttered to myself as I felt myself chewing on it again. I stood up and took a step towards my house.

Walking step by step along the tall brick wall bordering my house, I quickly hurried home. My head fell back as I felt the sun's rays drill through the top of my forehead. "Wow, today is really hot." I exclaimed as I lifted my head back. I opened my front door and took a step into the house.

Alan

Hopping up and down, I played double dutch with Emily and Megan. My hair dangled from side to side and I heard the beat of the ropes. I giggled, "Slow down guys," and popped up and down like popcorn. I moved my hand up toward my head.

Above my head went the skinny ropes and I ducked down so I wouldn't get hit. My chin nearly touched my

49

chest and I felt the ropes grow slower and slower. "Speed up a tiny bit, but not so fast!" I demanded as I prepared for a faster speed. They moved the ropes faster and faster.

Christina

As the black clouds concealed the radiant light of the sun, the lightning lit up the sky, and for a moment, just for a moment, you could see the terror on the faces of the people. You could hear the frightened children wail as their mom and dad squeezed them tight. They wished it would go away. Some of the children began to chant, "Rain, rain, go away, come again another day." Before they stopped, the thunder crashed as loud as ever.

Cameron

1st sentence—WHAT IS THE PICTURE?
include at least three details
begin with a verb or action phrase (1st paragraph)
begin with a prepositional phrase (2nd paragraph)

2nd sentence—SHOW NOT TELL ("SNT")
one body part
one sense

3rd sentence—THOUGHTS
use of quotation marks around thoughts of character

4th sentence—NEXT EXACT MOVEMENT

Level Four identifies and brings the issue of the use of quotation marks to the forefront.

Mini-Lesson

By this level, the students will begin experimenting with the actual placement of the direct quote. Their attempts may be clumsy and you may encounter samples such as *I was thinking, "I wish there was no school today"* and/or other variations on this sentence.

Focus their attention on the proper placement of commas and periods and teach them the correct way to use these kinds of punctuation. You might have a worksheet provided at this time, taken directly from a language arts textbook or workbook. We push them to use *I thought* as opposed to I was thinking, and this also takes time.

Turn their attention to the three sentences, listed below, that were prewritten on the board, and invite the class to discuss the various differences that they notice.

1. *"I wish there was no school today,"* I thought out loud tiredly.
2. I thought out loud tiredly, *"I wish there was no school today."*
3. I thought aloud, *"I wish there was no school today"* and plopped back on the bed.

Draw their attention to the three different places they can write a direct quotation and help them to pay attention to the proper placement of commas, quotation marks, and periods.

Do you remember the example of our boy sitting tiredly in his muggy classroom? Let's visit with him again.

After teaching the mini-lesson on quotations, have the class go back to this example since they are comfortable and familiar with it. Review the completed paragraph from the last time they worked on it and draw their attention to the third sentence.

> Slouching tiredly over his desk in a muggy classroom, the little boy quietly read his book. His neck ached and he could feel perspiration dribbling down his back. <u>He was thinking about recess and what he was going to do.</u> Slowly, he put the book down.

Ask the class to use their new knowledge of the expectations for the third sentence, and to rephrase it using a quotation. Allowing for discussion to take place, the class's end result might look like this:

> Slouching tiredly over his desk in a muggy classroom, the little boy quietly read his book.

> His neck ached and he could feel perspiration dribbling down his back. "What should I play at recess today?" he wondered softly. Slowly, he put the book down.

Your students will have a wonderful time as they begin to play with language. For those students who still experience difficulty, don't worry. Be patient, continue to give examples and individual tutorial help if necessary, and their enjoyment of language will come.

Review

Continue your daily procedures and weekly tests. You will see tremendous growth. Don't forget to remember the general rule of thumb about mini-lessons. Introduce two or three new mini-lessons within a single week. The remainder of the days should be simple reminders.

Together, your students and you will enjoy reading the paragraphs that begin to emerge.

Student Samples

How exciting to watch their written work change and grow. We have included three examples. All of these student samples reflect amazing growth, which is all the more impressive when we remember that many students begin as insecure writers.

> Slouching on the big blue couch, I was changing the channels while eating buttered popcorn. I heard the doggie door slam shut and my dog scampered in, looked at me and sniffed the popcorn. "Ryan did you get your homework done," my mom shouted as I crawled deeper into the couch. I jumped up and ran into my room so she wouldn't know I was watching T.V.
>
> Savanah

Drew

Clutching the bat with my feet in their place I was ready to hit a grand slam. My teeth were clenched together and I saw the ball flying toward me. "This is going to be a good hit" I whispered to myself. I swung the bat and hit the ball into left field.

After I hit the ball I ran around the bases with the bat in my hands. My waist turned to home base and I heard the umpire yell, "you're out." What happened?" I gasped. I went to the dugout and drank all my water.

Drew

Creeping to that slimy door,
Michael grabbed hold to his shirt,
his face full of terror. His eyes
looked at every wall that was
torn. "Who lives here," he thought
calling for someone that could
hear him. He gripped harder
on his clothes.

Near a vase, he saw a shadow
on the floor. He looked up with
fear. His hands shook fiercely and he could
see a silhouette on the ground.
"What is that or who is that," he
said with a horrible look. He then picked
up the vase, found a lizard crawl
out and was really relieved for
it was just an animal.

Ryan

CHAPTER 5

Level Five

Level Five adds character movement to the thoughts of the character so that we can continue to see the storyline moving.

Stretching my arms as high and wide as I could in the air, I was determined to catch the baseball. My waist twisted in a pretzel to the right as I ran and I could feel the sun pour down on me. I stumbled a little with my feet, made a desperate grab and yelled, "I got it!" The ball landed in my tightly held glove and I smiled in glee.

As I lowered my free hand down, I prepared to throw the ball back. My ears strained to hear where to throw the ball but I heard and saw nothing but the blinding sun. "Can I make the throw all the way," I pondered and I lifted the ball from my glove and cranked back my arm. I flung the ball forward with all my strength and threw it all the way to third.

Nicholas

Resting peacefully against a thick tree, I watched the sun slip behind the hills and let out a pleasurable sigh. My arms lay still in my lap and I smelled the strong aroma of carnations and daffodils in the air. "I feel like I've died and gone to heaven!" I whispered and shut my eyes in bliss. I stretched out my body and blinked my eyes open in time to watch the last golden drop drip behind the dark silhouette of the mountains.

Under the twinkling stars, I strolled home and took a deep breath of the cool night air. My hair fluttered around my face and I felt a pair of protruding eyes burn into the back of my head. "Oh no, someone is watching me!" I yelled and whipped around to see who was following me. I stared in shock into the laughing face of my sister.

Michelle

1st sentence—WHAT IS THE PICTURE

include at least three details

begin with a verb or action phrase (1st paragraph)

begin with a prepositional phrase (2nd paragraph)

2nd sentence—SHOW NOT TELL ("SNT")

one body part

one sense

3rd sentence—THOUGHTS

use of quotation marks around thoughts of character

add character movement

4th sentence—NEXT EXACT MOVEMENT

With the addition of character movement, you will see the students begin to have fun and begin bringing the characters to life.

Mini-Lesson

Ask the class to take a look at the example of the placement of quotes from Level Four. Keep the original format of the different quotes, prewritten on the board, but point out that the complexion of the sentence will change immediately as soon as character movement is added.

Pass out the teacher-made worksheet below, one to a group so that discussion is encouraged, with the following examples written.

Teacher-made worksheet

1) "I wish there was no school today," <u>I thought out loud tiredly as I yawned, stretched and wondered whether I should stay in bed.</u>

2) <u>As I yawned and stretched, I thought out loud tiredly,</u> "I wish there was no school today" <u>and wondered whether I could get away with staying in bed.</u>

3) <u>Yawning and stretching, I thought out loud tiredly,</u> "I wish there was no school today" <u>and immediately plopped back on the bed.</u>

Discuss student observations about each quotation placement, paying particular attention to what specific character movements were added.

Quick Dramatizations

You may decide to have a student model act this out to further emphasize the actions of the character. Remind students that details are what they are searching for in looking at character movement.

To secure this new knowledge in their minds, ask for a few student-volunteered quotations and write them on the board. The class should then help each other to create different possible character movements for each quotation.

Further dramatization of different student-volunteered suggestions at this point is fun, almost hilarious, and helps the students to understand that dialogue is not simply said but, rather, is accompanied by some type of action by the character.

Class Example

Now let's go back to our example about the boy reading his book.

> Slouching tiredly over his desk in a muggy classroom, the little boy quietly read his book. His neck ached and he could feel perspiration dribbling down his back. "What should I play at recess today?" he wondered softly. Slowly, he put the book down.

Paying close attention to the third sentence, ask the class to brainstorm together how character movement can be added. Accept any and all answers and have the students select their best possible choice.

The final result might now look like this.

> Slouching tiredly over his desk in a muggy classroom, the little boy quietly read his book. His neck ached and he could feel perspiration dribbling down his back. Watching the slow hands of the clock, he wondered softly, "What should I play at recess today?" and stretched his fingers. Slowly, he put the book down.

Having the students read aloud some of their written work will help to further reinforce and emphasize the placement of action to accompany thoughts. For those students who are still having some difficulties, these readings will prove invaluable and will be a safe, non-threatening way for them to hear what they are trying to achieve in their writing.

Student Samples

We have chosen five different student samples to better illustrate what you might be receiving. By this level, a minimum of two paragraphs can be expected, however, some students cannot complete two paragraphs due to various reasons. This is fine.

Standing in the snow, I shiver as I move around to keep warm. I rub my arms together, and stamp my feet, but I still feel the tingling of the snow. "Its all Mom's fault!" I think "If she hadn't made me wait for the bus, I wouldn't turn into a human popsicle!" All of a sudden I turn around to see the bus and everyone on it is squirming around, just like me.

Jessica

Bouncing on the bed up and down, left and right, sideways and around, I suddenly tripped on the covers. I plunged to the floor on my bottom, while my sister snickered silently. "Quiet, you little brat!" I snapped as I tried to ease the pain. I tried to get up but the pain was too powerful for me.

Ben

Rambunctiously kicking my blanket aside making my knees crack,I peered outside and saw a bright light that made my eyes shut as fast as they could i rubbed my eyes gently and unexpectedly felt fingers on my head pushing toward the ceiling. "Let me go!" I shouted fiercely, pushed the hand away, and slammed it on a nearby brick wall.I ran to my moms room without looking back and scrunched in beside her to get warm.

Kit

As I woke up to get out of bed my legs were filled with my full weight. and my back was aching. I squiggled around to get comfortable, dropped my legs, and sat up."If I stay like this I'll be late for school," I thought sleepily as I hurled myself off the bed. I burst out my room running briskly into the bathroom, to get ready for school.

Jason

Staring up at the grand sky, I saw huge puffs of pink clouds that looked like cotton candy, and it made me want to reach out for a bite, but I hesitated. My mouth watered as I miserably watched the wind blow it away. "Oh well," I sighed, "It's time to go home anyway." I looked down + disappointedly went home with cotton candy on my mind.

Whitney

CHAPTER 6

Level Six—Final Level

Hooray!

This last level is the most fun of all as students bring in all their ideas about dialoguing to the forefront. Different types of language, dialects, Standard English, and all the possible actions of the characters that go with dialogue make this enormous fun.

Eerie blackness surrounded me in the theater lit only by the screen as I dug down in my popcorn to get the bottom piece. My fingers were covered in grease and I felt them slip around in the box. As I licked my butter numbed lips, I wondered softly aloud. "When is this movie going to start?" I swiped a bit of popcorn off my lip with my tongue and settled down for the wait.

"Excuse me. Excuse me. I'm sorry. Excuse me." A line of last minute people stumble across me.

"Why do they wait so long? Why don't they plan their time better?"

"Oops, I accidentally kicked your soda over."

"That's okay," I mutter resentfully. I stared with blue eyes that are dark.

Around me, I heard the soft chatter of people and whisper of legs, clothes and food. I impatiently fidgeted in my seat and kept my eyes glued on the endless trivia. The opening music began and joyfully I heard people exclaim, "Finally. It's about time." Silently I agreed and relaxed to enjoy the show.

Nicholas

1st sentence—WHAT IS THE PICTURE

include at least three details

begin with a verb or action phrase (1st paragraph)

begin with a prepositional phrase (2nd paragraph)

2nd sentence—SHOW NOT TELL ("SNT")

one body part

one sense

3rd sentence—THOUGHTS

use of quotation marks around thoughts of character

add character movement

4th sentence—NEXT EXACT MOVEMENT

As you can see, nothing changes in Level Six. We do, however, add an emphasis on the addition and placement of a running dialogue between characters to move the action forward.

Where and how this dialogue is placed is the emphasis of Level Six.

Time Allotted

In the introductory mini-lesson of this last level, your pictures time might fly well past the one hour allotted since you will all be having such fun talking and acting out various written pieces. Be kind to yourself and allow for one hour. The students have an enormous sense of "talk story," and it is here that you will really hear their rich use of language.

Mini-Lesson

The use of dialogue helps to connect storyline and paragraphs, lend continuity to the story, and bring life to the characters.

During mini-lessons, it should be brought to the attention of the class that dialogue is used extensively in literature to move the storyline along. As you search through literature together, the use of dialogue and the important role it plays should be heavily emphasized.

Do you remember our example of the boy who is reading in a muggy classroom? We will now call him Michael and use him again to demonstrate three different ways that dialogue can be introduced.

1. Short, concise dialogue—"spurts"

> "Michael, it's time to stop reading."
>
> "Huh?"
>
> "You may stop reading now."
>
> "Now? . . ."
>
> "Yes. Now!"
>
> "Hooray!"

"Spurts" assumes that the storyline has already established who is talking so there will be no confusion as to who is saying what. Spurts are confined to exclamatory comments and should be kept short.

2. Dialogue using alternatives to "said" (Appendix I)

> "Michael, it's time to stop reading," the teacher whispered.
>
> "Huh?"
>
> "You may stop reading now." she repeated again.
>
> "Now? . . ."
>
> "Yes. Now!"
>
> "Hooray!"

In example 2, we have used the same dialogue from "spurts" and added on verbs which we call alternatives to "said." These quick verbs, and others such as moaned, yelled, whispered and many more, help the reader visualize exactly how the character is speaking. Rather than leave the reader to guess at the manner in which the dialogue is being spoken, it now becomes vividly clear. By adding in verbs, we can also better understand the individual personalities of each character.

3. Dialogue with character movement

"Michael, it's time to stop reading," the teacher whispered softly as she watched the class begin to get ready for recess. Wearily, she tucked a stray lock of damp hair behind her ear.

"Huh?" Michael blinked and stretched his feet out, clumsily knocking over the chair in front of him.

"You may stop reading now," she patiently repeated again.

"Now? . . ."

"Yes. Now!"

"Hooray!" With the sticky heat seemingly forgotten, Michael quickly ran out of the room in search of the recess field.

In example 3, we use the same "spurts" dialogue with the addition of alternatives to "said." You can see how our dialogue grows through the addition of verbs. We now add dialogue with character movement, adding yet another dimension to each character. We can see, with even more clarity, the actions of the characters and what is motivating them to act as they do.

By using a combination of all three types of dialogue explained above, your students will be able to make their characters breathe and come alive.

Further Mini-Lessons

Mini-lessons throughout this level should include concepts such as indenting each time a new character speaks, alternatives to "said," Appendix I, actions and purposes of character, and the placement of dialogue at the beginning, in between, and/or at the end of a pictures paragraph.

Placement of Dialogue

The issue of placement of dialogue at the beginning, in between, and/or at the end may seem confusing. Think back to Level Four when we first introduced quotations and their placement. Think back to Level Five when we delved deeper into the different ways that you could work with the placement of quotations and characters' movements.

Now, let's bring back the example of the boy, Michael, reading his book in the muggy classroom to help us see how we could fit our new knowledge of dialogue within the example.

Within one paragraph, we could move the dialogue to the end where it would fit comfortably, or move it to the beginning with appropriate adjustments made, depending upon the effect that we want to create.

Here is what one example of a finished product might look like. First, we'll show you the picture of Michael reading at his desk from Level Five, intact, as it was done in the previous chapter. We then take the same paragraph and add a running dialogue, reflective of Level Six, at the end of the paragraph.

(Sample A—Level Five)

Slouching tiredly over his desk in a muggy classroom, the little boy quietly read his book. His neck ached and he could feel perspiration dribbling down his back. Watching the slow hands of the clock, he wondered softly, <u>"What should I play at recess today?" and stretched his fingers.</u> Slowly, he put the book down.

(Sample B—Level Five with the addition of dialogue—Level Six)

Slouching tiredly over his desk in a muggy classroom, the little boy quietly read his book. His neck ached and he could feel perspiration dribbling down his back. Watching the slow hands of the clock, he wondered softly, "What should I play at recess today?" and stretched his fingers. Slowly, he put the book down.

"Michael, it's time to stop reading," the teacher whispered softly as she watched the class begin to get ready for recess. Wearily, she tucked a stray lock of damp hair behind her ear.

"Huh?" Michael blinked and stretched his feet out, clumsily knocking over the chair in front of him.

"You may stop reading now," she patiently repeated again.

"Now? . . ."

"Yes. Now!"

"Hooray!" With the sticky heat forgotten, Michael quickly ran out of the room in search of the recess field.

At this point, a second pictures paragraph can begin, moving the storyline forward even more.

Advice

As you conduct extensive and often hilarious mini-lessons, you will find students itching to write. Once they start, though, they often experience enormous difficulty and begin their classic lament: "I don't know how to begin. I don't know what to do." Have them try the following.

Write two paragraphs of pictures as usual, which by now is fairly easy, leaving a large space above their first paragraph, a large space in between the two paragraphs, and another space at the end of the second paragraph.

They now decide where they want to place their dialogue. Once they've done this, they write a "spurt." This is fairly easy for them and fun. Upon completion, we guide them to choose a few places where they want to show a bit of the character's personality and instruct them to add in a few alternatives to "said."

When they feel they are done, we ask them to review their dialogue one more time and choose one or two separate places that they want some character movement so that the reader can better understand what motivates each character.

Again, with time and patience, the students will begin to experience success and their stories will grow amazingly.

Think About

Students need time to experiment and to play with the different styles of dialogue so that they form a better understanding in their mind of how to fit it within their story.

At this final level, you will notice that students begin to gain much confidence and are beginning to show some sophistication in their written work. Individual differences and writing styles will shine through and your time will be spent largely on revisional ideas as opposed to grammatical concerns.

You may still see redundancies and awkward phrases as they work to connect their paragraphs and clarify their thoughts. These are natural, but you can help them through mini-lessons to edit their own problems. By doing this and gaining confidence, the students will also be able to conference with others.

As the students grow, so will you.

Student Samples

We have decided, at Level Six, to share with you two student sample selections. We hope you have as much fun reading them as we do.

> Practicing her piano sulkily, nine year old Sherry pushed the charcoal and ivory colored keys clumsily around. Her back slouched toward the ground and she heard the notes pour into her headphone that was attached to her piano. "This is so hard . . . ," Sherry thought and stared at her music book, trying to figure out the notes. Tears slowly flowed down her cheeks.
>
> "Sherry. Telephone."
>
> "Hello?" Sherry wearily replied into the phone. It was her friend Nicole inviting her down to the pool. Excitement flowed through her and she began jumping up and down.
>
> "Mom, may I please go down to the pool? Nicole is going with her mom and they invited me to join them," she begged.
>
> "You may go after you practice."
>
> "But mom, that'll take forever."

"I said you may go after you finish. No arguments."
Tearfully, she went back to practicing.

As she wiped her tears away, Sherry sat back down, sluggishly straightened her back and tried to play her piece again. Her shoulders trembled and shook up and down from the whimpering of her silent cries and she saw the hardest part of the music coming up. "Why does playing the piano have to be so time-consuming?" she moaned and repeated the hard part over again for the umpteenth time. She lifted her hair off her neck, wiped her cheeks, and began to concentrate with fierce determination.

Sherry

Plunking my feet into the cool water, I sat along the riverbank watching the ripples extend outward and wondered at myself. My mind swirled around, wrapped in dark colors, and I listened to the nearby birds and their echoing call. "What is wrong with me?" I wondered achingly. I lifted my head up towards the sky searching blindly for answers.

"Think of happy memories," I ordered myself with a false smile. "Think of my sister Lisa, and how she can sneeze and cough at the same time. Think of my family and how much fun we used to have."

The water continued to cool my feet.

I breathed the sweet smell of the earth, and noticed the beauty around me. The colors of the flowers, patches of blue, scuttling across the sky, the sound of crickets and my own water soaked toes.

Golden drops of sunlight poured into my eyes and they seemed to pull the golden parts of me out towards the sun. I pulled my feet out of the water, felt my face light up with a smile, and the adrenaline begin to flow through my body. "I guess I shouldn't linger on the past. I'll concentrate on the future." I thought with a slight smile. With mischievous eyes, my sister suddenly appeared, plopped on me, and we began to roll around the grass and giggle helplessly.

Michelle

CHAPTER 7

"Pictures" gives us a place to begin.

As a simple daily exercise, it gives us as teachers the confidence to understand where we can begin, the knowledge of how to build in a Spelling and Language Arts program, and yet empower the students with the ability to write from their own lives.

It helps us to connect the literature that we read to them and the literature that they read for themselves to their identities as writers who are writing about their own lives and thoughts.

"Pictures," however, can and should do much more than that.

Free Verse Poetry

When the students are fairly comfortable writing one or two paragraphs of pictures, discuss the components of free verse poetry and teach them about line breaks. Free verse poetry is fun to teach since there is no right or wrong answer. With the "pictures" paragraphs as a point of reference, the students can easily put their paragraphs into "poetic" form and play with the line breaks.

Let us show you how easily it can be done.

On a school field trip to the Iolani Palace, the residence of Lili'uokalani, the last Queen of Hawaii, the teacher instructed her students, then at Level Three, to write a picture about one aspect of what they had seen.

This is the end result from one young student.

> Looking at the quilt in Iolani Palace that Queen Lili'uokalani made when she was locked up, Sherry was surprised. Her arms crossed in front of her, her mouth opened like an O and she heard the guide explain the history of the quilt. She thought how beautiful it was. Going into King Kalakaua's bedroom, Sherry's friend Sheena held on to her arms.
>
> Sherry

Upon completion and correction of her picture, she then took her final product and turned it into a free verse poem. Here is her final result.

> Looking at the quilt
>
> in Iolani Palace
>
> which Queen Lili'uokalani made
>
> while locked up,
>
> Sherry's arms crossed
>
> and her mouth formed
>
> a silent O.
>
> Beautiful,
>
> she thought and moved
>
> towards King Kalakaua's
>
> bedroom.
>
> Sherry

Personal Essay Narrative

Personal Essay Narratives are fun. It is always easy for students to write about themselves and their lives once they see that their lives are full of things to write about.

Have them put together two or three pictures paragraphs and check for redundancy.

> My grandmother's attic is concealed by a blanket of dust. Two broken chairs lying almost as one big heap

sit noiselessly in the farthest corner. I see leaks in the roof where drops of water are raining down into an over-filled pot and I try to block it up with my finger. It brings back memories of that one summer and I start cleaning up.

"Whitney, what are you doing there?" I hear my mom calling out to me but my mind wanders back to the past.

"Why was it so painful? Why did everyone tell me to try and be brave? Couldn't they see I needed to feel and act out my pain?"

"Whitney?"

"I'm up in the attic."

"What are you doing up there?"

In my mind I can see her downstairs, hands on her hips with that look on her face.

"I'll be down soon. In a few minutes." I know she'll shrug, think I'm spending too much time here but that's okay. In this attic, with its memories, I can heal.

Whitney

Realistic Fiction

After students write two or three pictures paragraphs, making sure to use dialogue, ask them to go through what they've written and give their characters fictitious names. Focus their attention on the use of "he" and/or "she" instead of "I." You will quickly see that, in an instant, their piece has become a realistic fiction.

This young student needed to write a realistic fiction for a class-assigned magazine project. Taking the characters from her Archie comics, she quickly created a storyline that had in fact happened to her. Using her knowledge of the basic format of pictures, she was able to come up with her finished story, shown on the next page.

One Night

One night, three good friends named Betty, Veronica and Midge were getting ready to play hide and seek. As Midge counted "Twenty One Fingers" to start the game, they could hear the wind blowing the grass around them. Midge was out, so she began counting to ten.

"One, two . . . ten! Ready or not, here I come!" she yelled. Betty and Veronica were both nervous because it was so dark.

They ran around behind trees that were in straight rows and looked in front, then back. WHOOP! WHOOSH! Veronica had slipped in fresh mud, all the way from her legs to her bottom and up to her waist. To Betty, she looked like a half brown human.

"Oh Betty, please help me walk to my house and get all washed up." Veronica wailed.

"Sure." They ran a quick two blocks to get to Veronica's house.

Veronica rubbed up and down, back to right. She did that all over, until she felt clean. They ran back and upon seeing them, Midge asked them where they had been and told them she couldn't find them at all since their hiding place was so good. Betty told her what happened and Midge put her arm around Veronica. "That's okay Veronica, it happens to the best of us."

Stepping carefully as they walked, Betty, Veronica, and Midge looked all around them and below not wanting to step or fall in mud. They clasped their hands together, and felt the smoothness of each other's skin.

WHOOP! WHOOSH! Oh no, Betty fell in the mud.

Sherry

Integration into Content Curriculum

"Pictures" works well with integration. Writing in all curriculum areas may seem difficult but there are many ways that this can be done. Here are some simple beginning ideas. We're sure you can add many of your own wonderful ideas.

Reading.   Read a story, ask students to visualize, then have them write a picture predicting what will happen next. Any picture book or chapter book will do. Since the format is already understood, this is quite self-explanatory.

We've had students working independently, or in groups, or as partners. We notice that when we ask the students to visualize and focus on either what will happen to the character or what will the character most probably do next, the task is much easier. If the task is difficult, just remember to ask the students to illustrate their thoughts.

Science.   Have them write one or two paragraphs about what they observe. A variation of this might be to personify one of the animals they are currently studying.

> While swimming inside a tide pool, I saw a starfish gracefully strolling on the sand. I felt the water tickle my nose and reached out my hand to slowly grab it. "I wonder how it feels to touch a starfish?" I thought and noticed I was only about five inches away. I grabbed a leg and it broke, but surprisingly, I saw something grow out of its leg very, very, very, . . . slowly.
>
> Maria

Social Studies.   Have the students illustrate one aspect of history carefully, and write several paragraphs about it.

Art.   Tie the art in with Social Studies or another content area.

One variation might be to illustrate and cut it up jigsaw puzzle style. Did you know that the creation of the jigsaw puzzle is part of our American history? Have them then write a picture from the character's point of view to accompany the puzzle.

To demonstrate, here are two student examples.

There I was, warning people from farm to farm about the Revolutionary War. My chest was tucked low near the back of the horse and I spotted a young boy in the field. "Hey, you over there," I yelled while waving my hands furiously in the air. The boy came running towards me with a musket in his hand ready to fire.

He made a stop when he reached me, stood there and I watched him closely from my seat on my horse. My thighs leaned gently on the horse's side and I could feel my heart thumping. "You have to warn your parents about the war," I yelled out losing patience. Flinging myself down on my horse, I got ready to go.

Michelle

illustration by Michelle

Hiking up hills and down, I was searching for food to hunt for my supper. Both my hands gripped tightly to my six foot rifle and I could feel the heartbeat of a creature coming towards me through my blood. "Wa-hoo creature, I'm ready to invite you to my table for supper," I thought humorously as I began to kneel. I had my right pointer finger ready to pull on the trigger.

Through my keen sense, I heard twigs crackling. My arms shifted left to right, back and forth from the weight of the rifle and I could hear my heart begin to pound with fear. Suddenly, I saw a raccoon run in front of me rapidly and I thought, "Yes, supper. A delicious raccoon." I pulled the trigger and shot it in the head.

Maria

illustration by Roseller

Music.   Play a piece of classical music, such as one by Beethoven, and then discuss his life. Ask students to begin drawing or sketching what memories the music evokes in them. Upon completion, give them time to discuss and reflect. Then ask them to write pictures about it. Here are some student examples.

Darkness completely surrounded me and I watched sadly as the rose began to slowly sink in the water, twisting my heart with pain. A giant knot formed in my stomach and I felt tears slide down my cheeks, slowly, and fall into the puddle in which the rose drowned in. "The rose is dying" I thought, lifting my head up as if giving a silent prayer to God. I sadly put my head back down to watch.

Before my eyes, the rose began to wither away, it's petals slowly sinking to the bottom of the puddle. The pain in my throat ached terribly and my eyesight was a blur of colors. "Why do I have to watch?" I cried in my head while trembling all over. I slowly picked up the remains of the dead rose.

Michelle

With a loud crash, Beethoven slammed his hands on the piano. He looked furious and his hands were in the air ready to slam down on the piano again so hard it would probably crack a knuckle. He thought to himself, "My music is the greatest!" After awhile, he began to play a sad song.

As he played, a girl began to cry. She had a sad expression on her face and her eyes were so droopy that it seemed she would soon fall asleep. She sleepily yawned and thought, "This is beautiful." She slowly drifted off.

Savanah

As I lay on the soft sand with water touching my feet, I saw darkness everywhere. The water came and brushed my feet while I heard the whistling wind. "This is a beautiful place," I thought to myself as a shooting star flew by. Slowly, I moved my body into a sitting position.

Moving upwards with my hair blowing in the wind, I began to see fish. I could see their mouths open and close while my toe gave me a sudden sharp pain. "I wonder if the fish will go away?" I wondered as I saw the crab reaching out his long claw towards me again.

Angela

Celebrations. Holiday memories.   Begin with I REMEMBER . . . and tell students to write a picture. Have students create a card with the illustrated picture as well as the written picture and it will be a memory treasured forever by parents. The I REMEMBER . . . format can be used for most holidays and works well to help students connect their own life experiences with content areas.

CHAPTER 8

Last Thoughts

Pictures does not address the wide variety of writing styles or genres. Because of its daily exercise format, however, it does give both teacher and student a good strong beginning point for where to start in their quest to develop as writers, and as teachers of writers.

Writing is a lonely activity. We become vulnerable and, at times, insecure about what we see and how to help. It takes time, effort, and a letting go of insecurities.

We have found it helpful to work with colleagues; this has brought about much conversation about writing. We use these meeting times to discuss how our students are doing in comparison to others, what we consider to be deficient skills as we've observed our students, our grading concerns, and help needed in potential mini-lesson areas.

We have learned that we are wonderful resources for each other and know much more than we think. Once faced with student samples, we have found that all teachers are able to share at least one area of concern that they feel needs to be addressed.

Pictures allow each student their own dignity. They learn to trust themselves and understand that good writing comes from within. They learn to conference with purpose and what tools to use when help is needed.

Through Pictures, students now gain the self-confidence to fly.

WHAT DO YOU DO IF . . .

Whenever we purchase something new, no matter how careful we are, we eventually come up with a problem. With our car, it was how to open the trunk. With our computer, it was everything after turning it on. With our daughter's first bike, it was putting it together. With our new television, it was learning how to make use of all its features.

Even with the best-laid plans, problems occurred. We noticed that the first thing we searched for was a brochure or book. Perhaps the clearest example of how to use brochures to help ourselves was our quest for a book to help us with our computer.

The book that came with our software didn't speak to us. We found it difficult and confusing to sift through and eventually admitted defeat. We went to a local bookstore and emerged with "WORD FOR DUMMIES."

After thinking through our problems and how we solve them, we decided to create this section called WHAT DO YOU DO IF . . . We hope it helps you to better understand any problem areas that surface.

1. If students forget to follow the format . . .

Mini-lessons taught by the teacher should always begin with a review of the format. Have the format clearly written, laminated and posted so that all students can refer to it. Some teachers prefer to simply paste it inside the tablet for students. Remind all the students that, just like a recipe, they can add and experiment; however, they must stick to the basic format.

2. **If students forget the date . . .**

Quickly make this an issue, because writing the date should become automatic on all papers. Grades can be lowered if the date is missing. Students can be asked to stay in at recess and discuss why they didn't write the date. Their paragraph can be refused for acceptance if a date isn't on it.

3. **If students don't know what a sentence is . . .**

We have noticed that many students are confused about how phrases, incomplete sentences, and complete sentences differ. We have the students read orally so they can hear the flow of language, and we read and repeat what they have written for them. This needs to be done so they can hear where the voice drops to indicate an ending. You might also want to point out that each sentence should have a subject and a verb before it can be considered complete.

4. **If the student is new to the class . . .**

Since the paragraph embraces a concept of four sentences, it is actually quite easy to learn. You might have a peer tutor the student or simply give him or her extra help on the side.

5. **If students begin the first sentence with "I" . . .**

Teach a mini-lesson on specific ways to begin each sentence. Connect their writing strongly to literature and help students to explore how authors begin their stories and storylines.

You might tie in "grammar" as we did, for example, by asking them to begin with a prepositional phrase or a verb phrase.

6. **If students don't finish . . .**

We like to make heavy use of a clock and draw attention to "time on task." "Pictures" is not a complete story, nor should it take the place of a finished piece. Rather, it should be looked at as writing exercises to free the mind and to be done quickly.

Revision and the process of moving what was produced in the exercise into a potential story is what will take time and this is where a longer block of writing workshop would probably become needed eventually.

7. **If students take too long to draw . . .**

A clock is necessary because it is used to establish a time limit to help the students not draw for too long a time. Of course, some students will have special needs and more time will be necessary for them.

A few students might demonstrate a need to draw only in the beginning, as this will be their way of "writing" initially. Others might demonstrate a need to draw in clear detail to help clarify the details in their minds.

These are issues that you will need to think through. What we do is ask the students to prepare, in their mind, what picture they could draw and write about, as homework the night before. This ensures, usually, that a picture is ready to be physically drawn and that a minimal amount of time is spent thinking "What should I draw and write about?"

For the few students who cannot hurry themselves along, we ask them to draw the night before so that class time can be devoted only to the writing.

8. **If students ramble past four sentences . . .** ·

Keep nudging and reminding them that these are exercises and should be confined to four sentences. When necessary, we have numbered each sentence for them. When it seems almost impossible to accomplish this because the student continues to ramble, we have asked him or her to write four sentences on four separate, clearly defined lines. It should resemble a grocery list. Once students can demonstrate this, we move them back into paragraph form.

9. **If student writings do not give enough details . . .**

We ask them to count on their fingers until they reach three and make sure that three details are in their first sentence. When students are stuck, we cue them by asking about their picture and generally focus our questioning cues on "What are you doing?, Where are you?, Who are you with?, What kind of day was it?, How do you feel?, and What part of the day or season is it?"

10. If there are not enough "show" details . . .

If we are looking for even more "show," we go back to dramatization. There is a tendency to string adjectives together to "show" details. Give an example, such as the description of an apple, and ask them which of the two versions sounds better.

Sample A—The good, crunchy, delicious, cold, crispy apple was juicy.

Sample B—The apple was crisp and crunchy and when I bit into it, the juice spit in my eye.

After sharing examples of adjectives strung together, we again discuss "show" and allow time for discussions. We give an example, such as riding on the bus, and ask students to "show" us on the bus.

Riding on the crowded bus, riding in the back of the bus, riding in the middle of the bus next to the lady with a large shopping bag that was banging on my knee are all examples of how to extend and develop the concept of "show."

We scrutinize closely, looking for the little details that will help to "show" what is happening. We comb through our literature as well, copying down samples in our writer's notebook that we feel best illustrates "show" details.

11. If the fourth sentence doesn't make sense . . .

We rely heavily upon drama at this point to help students have a clear understanding of the actions of the character. We usually ask students to randomly act out certain pictures and then "slow-motion" the last sentence. Upon occasion, we'll use the TV and press the pause button and discuss the fourth sentence from that point of view.

12. If their picture and text don't match . . .

This has actually happened. We find it amazing and extremely intriguing. We focus their attention on the picture they have drawn and ask them to tell us about it. Then we direct their attention to their written work and help them to see that both must match.

13. If the first sentence is hard to begin . . .

Once you ask the student "What is the picture and what are you doing?" it is not that difficult for the student to begin writing. Usually, it is a fear of being wrong that causes the hesitation. Reassure the student that his or her attempts will be valued. Giving the student a phrase to begin with is also extremely helpful and provides some modeling.

14. If the student says "I'm not thinking of anything" (the third sentence) . . .

Help them to see that we all do in fact think of things. Go back with the student to "revisit" his picture together and retrace his thoughts with him. Usually, this is all that's needed.

15. If students run out of ideas . . .

Once the initial waterfall of ideas pours out of students, they begin wailing that "I don't have anything more to write about, my life is not exciting, I can't think anymore." Teach them about beginning a writer's journal and through mini-lessons make them aware of the world around them. Encourage them to write down lists of intriguing words, interesting phrases, ideas that pop into their heads, curious moments, and so on. Teach them to be constantly on the lookout for ideas. You might even want to begin a class list of potential writing ideas.

16. If students cannot seem to write the first sentence well . . .

Take a week's break and stop pictures. Each day, ask your students to look closely at literature and find examples of the first sentence. Make sure you remind them to look for three actions and rich details. Have them keep a log in their writer's notebook for easy reference and, with time, they will become more familiar with good writing.

17. If you just can't find the time to do all four sentences . . .

Be kind to yourself and understand that schedules are difficult. The school day has many demands and there will be many moments when finding even thirty minutes is difficult. If this seems to be the case on a constant basis, you might want to try to concentrate on only one sentence each week.

Have students work on only one teacher-designated sentence every day for one week. If you do sentence one on week one, sentence two on week two, and so forth, you will strengthen their knowledge of how to write that type of sentence. When you finally bring it all together, they might be much more comfortable, as well as excited, to see the final product.

18. If their vocabulary is limited . . .

Write common words such as *walk, cold, pretty, nice, good, put, leave* on a chart and ask students for their input. Encourage wide use of thesauruses as well as looking through their literature.

Discuss the use of verbs and adverbs and elicit as many responses as you can from the students under categories such as running, sitting, and playing.

Write these words large and place the word charts you have created on a bulletin board for easy reference.

19. If you want to use Pictures as a writing "tool" in writing workshop towards revision . . .

If you want to explore different types of writing "tools" towards revision . . .

If you have completed all six levels and want to go further . . .

We are currently trying to address these questions and many more through Book II: Writing After Pictures.

While this section may not answer all your concerns, we hope it answers the large majority of them. When all else fails, please don't forget to dialogue with other teachers. We are a large community of thinkers. Remember that we are, when all else fails, our own best resources.

APPENDIX A
Suggested Mini-Lesson Ideas

1. Where to set up books
2. How to set up tablet

   Left side—Illustration

   Right side—Written
3. Skill folder—purposes and how to use it
4. Basic format of pictures
5. Three details in the first sentence
6. Picture must match text
7. Check for tense agreement
8. Check revision and spelling
9. Beginning with verb phrases
10. Beginning with prepositional phrases
11. Searching for higher vocabulary
12. Making use of the thesaurus
13. Searching through literature
14. Connecting to literature
15. Connecting to a second paragraph
16. Moving on to the next level
17. Grading policies—nothing lower than a "C"
18. Don't begin first sentence with a subject
19. Watch transitions
20. Make use of word banks around the room
21. Ask a neighbor for help with following format

22. Always have an idea ready to write

23. Turn on "television" and pause—that's an idea

24. Integrate into curriculum
    - reading—ask them to write a picture when you stop a story to predict what will happen next
    - art—ask them to write a "picture" to illustrate a point they want to make or something they have drawn
    - subject areas—ask them to write a picture within research
    - Language arts—ask them to write a picture within different genres

25. Take pictures and move them into realistic fiction

26. Take pictures and move them into free verse poetry

27. Take pictures and move them into personal essay narrative

28. Take pictures and point out sequential nature of pictures and apply it to writing for directions

29. Read samples every day and get class accustomed to subject grading and evaluation

30. Integrate computers into pictures. Have them type periodically to get comfortable with typing text straight into a computer without having it pre-written.

31. Spelling—drop "e"

32. Spelling—double consonant words

33. Suffixes

34. Prefixes

35. Endings of words

36. Subject verb agreements

37. Parts of speech

38. Vowel rules

39. "Wh" words

40. Their, there, they're

41. Contractions

42. Hyphenations

43. Abbreviations

44. Metaphors

45. Personification

46. Similes

47. Transitional words

48. Use of commas

49. Conferencing

50. Where to put periods

51. What is a sentence

52. Revision—look again

53. Editing

54. Editing identification marks

55. Moving into a second paragraph

56. Redundancy

57. Dialogue

58. Alternatives to "said"

59. Focusing on "senses"

APPENDIX B
Level One

Pictures

(LEFT) DRAW——(RIGHT) WRITE

1. WHAT IS THE PICTURE?

2. SHOW NOT TELL "SNT"—

   **HANDS AND FEET

3. THOUGHTS

4. NEXT EXACT MOVEMENT

APPENDIX C
Frequently Mispelled Words

	A	B	C	D	E
1	a lot	because	cafeteria	different	easy
2	add	before	coming (15)		especially
3	after	being	could		
4	always	believe (10)			
5	apologize	breathe			
6	are	breath			
7		build			

	F	G	H	I	J
1	friend (20)	girl	head		
2		guard	heard		
3			high (25)		
4			hour		

	K	L	M	N	O
1	know	leaving	making		our
2		light	minute		
3		little (30)			

	P	Q	R	S	T
1	peace		right (40)	said	taught
2	piece (35)			should	teach
3	please			stomach	THEIR things
4	practice			sweet	over THERE
5	pretend			sweat	THEY'RE (50)
6	pretty				thought
7					threw
8					through
9					tonight
10					touch (55)
11					tough
12					trouble
13					tomorrow

	U	V	W	X	Y
1			watch		yesterday (70)
2			whale (60)		
3			WHAT		
4			WHEN		
5			WHERE		
6			WHO		
7			WHY		
8			would		
9			write		
10			went		
11			were		

TEST—once a week

70 words total

vocabulary word list given each week—TEST

Appendix D
Past, Present, Future—Tense

**USE YOUR CHART and write 3 sentences for each word.
**watch out for TRICKS

(example: BAKE)

past tense   (I baked a cake.)

present tense   (I am baking a cake.)

future tense   (I will bake a cake.)

WALK:

1. _____

2. _____

3. _____

WATCH:

1. _____

2. _____

3. _____

PLAY:

1. _____

2. _____

3. _____

TALK:

1. _____
2. _____
3. _____

EAT:

1. _____
2. _____
3. _____

WRITE:

1. _____
2. _____
3. _____

THINK:

1. _____
2. _____
3. _____

RUN:

1. _____
2. _____
3. _____

TEACH:

1. _____
2. _____
3. _____

Appendix E
Skill Folder a
Choice 1 Alphabet Chart

A	B	C
1)	1)	1)
2)	2)	2)
3)	3)	3)
4)	4)	4)
5)	5)	5)
6)	6)	6)
7)	7)	7)
8)	8)	8)
9)	9)	9)
10)	10)	10)
11)	11)	11)
12)	12)	12)
13)	13)	13)
14)	14)	14)
15)	15)	15)
16)	16)	16)
17)	17)	17)
18)	18)	18)
19)	19)	19)
20)	20)	20)
21)	21)	21)
22)	22)	22)
23)	23)	23)
24)	24)	24)
25)	25)	25)
26)	26)	26)
27)	27)	27)

Choice 1 Skill List

	Date	Genre	Skill List
1			
2			
3			
4			
5			
6			
7			
8			
9			
10			
11			
12			
13			
14			
15			
16			
17			
18			
19			
20			
21			
22			
23			
24			
25			
26			
27			
28			
29			
30			
31			
32			
33			
34			
35			

APPENDIX F
Skill Folder b
Choice 2 Skill Chart (blank)

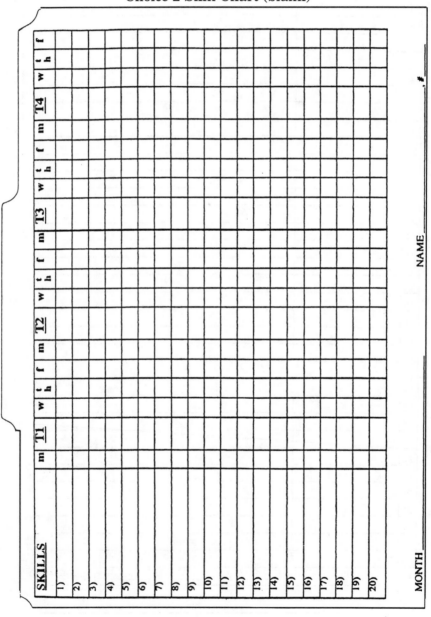

Choice 2 Skill Chart

SKILLS	m	T1	w	t/h	f	m	T2	w	t/h	f	m	T3	w	t/h	f	m	T4	w	t/h	f
1) date and name																				
2) follows proper format																				
3) 1st sentence - 3 actions																				
4) 2nd sentence-conjunction																				
5) 3rd sentence-thoughts																				
6) 4th sentence-10 words+																				
7) uses "show" details																				
8) Do not use -- Then																				
9) higher grade words																				
10) indent																				
11) Do not repeat words																				
12) Capital letters																				
13) Proper spelling																				
14) periods																				
15) space between words																				
16) quotation marks																				
17) commas																				
18) alternatives to "said"																				
19) said plus adverb																				
20) indents-new ch. speaks																				
21) dialogue w/ch. movement																				
22) dialogue-diff. parts sentence																				
23) present tense																				
24) past tense																				
25) future tense																				
26) question mark																				
27) exclamation point																				
28) apostrophe																				

NAME _____

MONTH _____

Appendix G
Descriptors

Hand Movement Descriptors

glued	touching	pointing	grabbing
cemented	wobbling	shaking	jabbing
frozen	relaxing	hugging	stretching
stuck	tucked	squeezing	outstretched
nailed	crisscrossed	slapping	shivering
wavering	receiving	jerking	fiddling
gripped	clapping		

Feet Movement Descriptors

nailed	kicking	swaying	drilled
balanced	heavy	clinging	poking
stuck	tiptoeing	leaping	tingling
shivering	twisting	squeaking	bending
burning	jumping	gliding	aching
flip-flopping	pointing	tapping	
swinging	balancing	hammered	

Body Descriptors

gnarly legs	knobby knees	splotches	varicose vein
spindly legs	elephantitis	short legs	stubby toes
pumped up	high arch	stork neck	gargantuan
spider nails	blistery heel	calloused	tattooed
jelly belly	bowlegged	pudgy	chicken skin
love handles	fair-skinned	dough-boy	
thin muscles	hairy legs	marshmallow	

Face Descriptors

liver spots	eyes twinkle	wrinkly	impish/impy
square jaw	silver-haired	plucked eyes	dumbo ears
tooth chip	flaring nose	painted lips	almond eyes
onion breath	scrunched	dimpled	thick lips
grind teeth	prickly hair	baby soft	baggy eyes
puffed cheek	freckled	silly grin	
crooked nose	sun-baked	pouting	

Mood Descriptors

blustery	morose	peaceful	heaven sent
sulky	punkish	sunshiny	calm
slothful	melancholy	light	placid
mopish	foreboding	breezy	carefree
gloomy	deafening-silence	breathless	spiritual
dark		awe-inspiring	
sullen	serene	sun-soaked	

Ground Descriptors

moist	sloshy	porous	rugged
damp	dusty	slippery	thorny
spongy	barren	glassy	carpet
rocky	rich	oven baked	sinking
wave of grass	volcanic	waving heat	splotches
lush	pebbly	earthwormy	
crumbly	sandy	razor sharp	

Sky Descriptors

clear	rainbow hued	angry	heavy
light	colored	turbulent	foreboding
airy	darkness	happy	liquid sun
windy	deep purple	rainy	puffy
endless	blackness	blustery	touching
stormy	bluish ocean	starry	
hidden	mirror (sea)	dripping	

APPENDIX H
Prepositions

---

about	behind	inside	over
above	below	into	through
across	beside	near	to
after	between	of	toward
along	by	off	under
among	down	on	until
around	for	onto	up
at	from	out	with
before	in	outside	

APPENDIX 1
Said Verbs

contradicted
heaved
stared
rested
announced
wondered
protested
beckoned
commanded
demanded
quavered
insulted
complimented
twinkled
justified
resented
smiled
ached
lied
warned
retorted
implied
sneered
snobbed
hesitated

shouted
screamed
choked
puzzled
panted
gulped
frowned
finished
worried
faltered
persisted
panted
complained
amazed
decided
prompted
relaxed
counted
yelped
trilled
muttered
grumbled
fidgeted
shook
twittered

breathed
gasped
snapped
persisted
stammered
ended
exclaimed
pronounced
pressed
smiled
presumed
asked
inquired
listened
chuckled
wondered
coaxed
whistled
mumbled
screeched
sighed
trembled
implored
wailed
gasped

exclaimed
teased
sang
suggested
grumbled
snapped
jumped
frowned
replied
sobbed
whispered
cried
yelled
screamed
yawned
begged
moaned
giggled
laughed
answered
questioned
prayed
pleased
watched

APPENDIX J
Said Verbs Plus Adverbs

excitedly	fiercely	constantly	imposingly
silently	pathetically	wonderingly	honestly
drowsily	reluctantly	grumpily	prayerfully
courageously	hoarsely	tiredly	questioningly
thoughtfully	testily	grouchily	commandingly
pleasurably	shortly	happily	snappily
crossly	seriously	promptly	

INDEX

About the Authors

Hal and Michelle Takenishi have their Master's Degree in Education with an emphasis on reading and writing.

Hal has been teaching for 12 years in both secondary and elementary schools. Between putting on reading events, beginning a kinderbuddy program with his students and the kindergarten children, in-servicing teachers on writing, and actively serving on various committees working toward the goal of literacy for all, he continues researching and learning.

Michelle has taught elementary school for 15 years and is a part-time lecturer at the University of Hawaii in the College of Education. She is a recipient of the Professional Best Leadership Award and was listed in the Who's Who of American Education. She has conducted workshops on reading and writing, and helped build a network of teachers who are held together by the common bond of wanting to learn more.